TREASURE HUNTS

by
Harriet Hope Green
Dr. Sue Gillespie Martin

illustrated by Gerald Melton

Cover by Gerald Melton

Copyright © Good Apple, Inc., 1983

ISBN No. 0-86653-115-7

Printing No. 98765432

GOOD APPLE, INC.
BOX 299
CARTHAGE, IL 62321-0299

Printed in the United States of America at Patterson Printing, Benton Harbor, Michigan.

DEDICATIONS

To my mother, Dorothy Stiden Gillespie, who read aloud to me every day during my childhood, introducing me to the joys of literature.

To my family and friends who fill my treasure chest with love, support and patience.

CLASSIC LITERATURE FOR CHILDREN

The strongest thread defining the pattern of a literary classic is "staying power." A classic outlives fads and fancy in both theme and style. It is just as genuinely loved by the current generation as it was by the previous one. Furthermore, it yields to no boundary of time or geography. A classic eloquently speaks a universal tongue.

Children's literary classics, those books either written for children or adopted by children, have as much endurance as their adult counterparts. *Treasure Hunts* contains ten stories loved by children, selected on the basis of their power of endurance. The source of their collective strength is the mighty combination of fantasy, adventure and heroism.

Treasure Hunts makes its escape into fantasy by tumbling down a rabbit's hole, catching a boat on the high seas and getting all caught up in a cyclone. *The Wizard of Oz* and *Alice in Wonderland and Through the Looking Glass* were exquisitely designed for children. *Gulliver's Travels*, on the other hand, was satirically patterned for adults but adopted by children because of its highly imaginative nature. Furthermore, what generation of children would not be attracted by the limitless possibilities of a visit to such places as Lilliput, Wonderland and Emerald City? In addition, these books give the child an opportunity to walk hand in hand with eccentrics like the Mad Hatter, the Wicked Witch and the Queen of Hearts and hobnob with Munchkins, Yahoos and Winged Monkeys.

Every child needs a hero. Most of them last a lifetime but some last for generations. This is the case with King Arthur, Robin Hood and Mark Anthony. All of these figures display one or more of the classic heroic characteristics - courage, loyalty, strength, vitality, cleverness and defender of both truth and justice.

King Arthur is one of the most enduring heroes in literature. His devotion to the equality of the Round Table and justice for his countrymen combined with his physical strength and mental courage make him a hero for all seasons.

Robin Hood, on the other hand, had equal vitality, strength and courage but possessed a cleverness that served him well. He tricked the Sheriff of Nottingham with his bold disguises and won the day for everyman. He is a hero whom children could pattern themselves after in their imaginations.

Mark Anthony, protege of Julius Caesar, proves through words and deeds to be a hero who worships at the altar of loyalty. During the story, included here as a challenging extension into more demanding literary forms, Mark Anthony displays incredible courage, cleverness and loyalty. He stands up to everyone, cleverly convinces the people that Caesar loved them and remains true to his friend in the face of an angry mob.

Heidi and Tom Sawyer maintain their classic appeal because they are children who dared to live out their fantasies in an adult world. Tom interacts with criminals, orphans and proper elders who help enrich his daring schemes. Heidi bestows compassion on a cripple, an old man, and a blind grandmother and enchants them all with her cheer.

With pirates, shipwrecks, and buried treasure, the most physical adventure in *Treasure Hunts* is *Treasure Island*. The stakes are high and the reward is golden. *Robinson Crusoe* is a mental adventure matching man's wit and problem-solving ability against nature. Survival is the prize for winning the game.

THE ADVENTURES OF TOM SAWYER

MARK TWAIN

THE OLD WHITEWASH-THE-FENCE TRICK

OBJECTIVES:

    1.   To encourage students to use their imagination.

    2.   To encourage each child to experience the "whitewashing the fence" scene from the kids' points of view rather than just Tom's point of view.

MATERIALS: Objects from home, a bucket, a paintbrush, and two straw hats.

PROCEDURE:

    1.   Assign the whitewashing episode to be read by the students.

    2.   Discuss the persuasive action of the episode based on the following Twain quotation:

    "...in order to make a man or boy covet a thing it is only necessary to make the thing difficult to attain." (Be sure to define "covet.")

    3.   Review with the students the list of things Tom collected from the kids in return for a chance to whitewash the fence, such as an apple, twelve marbles, tadpoles, a brass doorknob, a key, a dog collar and a kite.

    4.   Ask each student to go home and find **one** item that will fit into a pocket to bring to class to be used as a bargaining tool with Tom Sawyer for a chance at the fence. Stress that students should use their imagination when selecting items that they think will really persuade Tom. Whatever the item, however, baseball cards, candy bar, etc., each student must prepare a short verbal selling point as to why Tom should want the item.

    5.   The next day the class should be divided into groups of two with one person playing Tom's role and one person playing the kid's role. Then, one group at a time, the entire class will see and hear the kid show Tom the item he has in his pocket and tell Tom what it is good for, what its value is and why he should want to exchange it for a chance to whitewash the fence. (Tom should wear a straw hat and have a bucket and brush as a prop, whereas the kid should have a straw hat and whatever item he has selected in his pocket.)

    6.   The procedure should then be repeated with all the students playing Tom switching to the kid's role and vice versa so that every student gets an opportunity to experience the scene from both points of view.

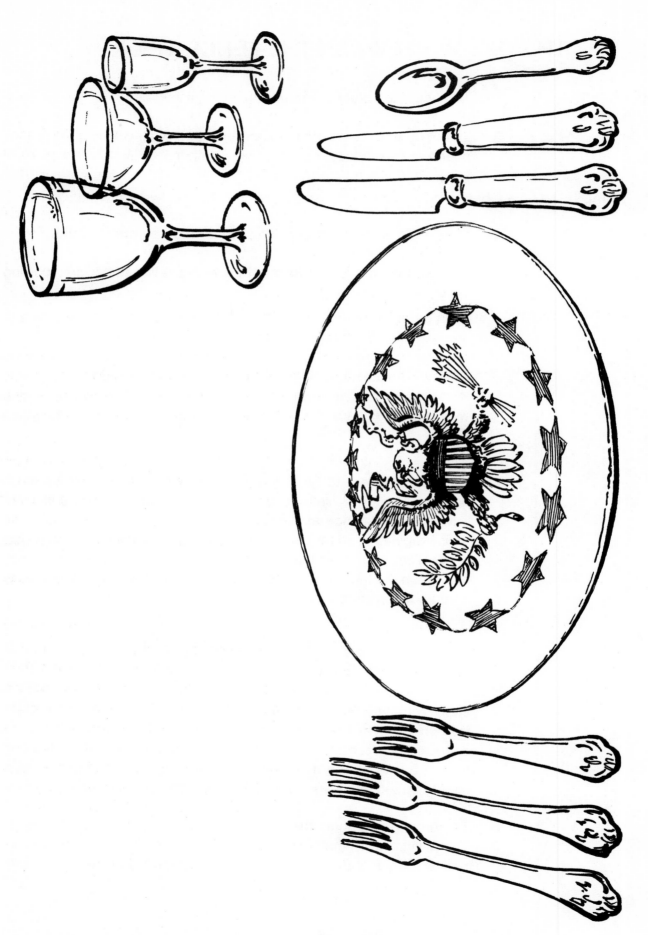

THE WIDOW DOUGLAS' FINISHING SCHOOL

OBJECTIVE: To give each student the opportunity to relate to how hard it was for Huck to change from uncivilized to civilized in social graces.

MATERIALS: Books, 4 dinner plates, 4 dinner forks, 4 knives, 4 salad bowls, 4 water glasses, 4 spoons, 4 salad forks, 4 napkins, 4 coffee cups and saucers.

PROCEDURE:

1. Assign the final chapters of the book, including the episode between Huck and Tom where Tom persuades Huck to return to the Widow Douglas.

2. Discuss how difficult it was for Huck to live within the rigid framework that the Widow Douglas demanded by using the following quotation:
    "The widder wouldn't let me smoke, she wouldn't let me gape, nor stretch, nor scratch before folks..."

3. Tell the students they will all be enrolled for one day at the Widow Douglas' Finishing School where they will learn to walk with correct posture, make verbal introductions properly and correctly set a table for a formal dinner. In this way they may be able to empathize with Huck.

4. Ask each student to put a book on his/her head and **one at a time** get up from the desk, go to the front of the room, turn and walk back to the desk without letting the book fall. Remind each student to stand up straight and smile.

5. Ask for four volunteers each to come forward and arrange a place setting for a formal dinner.

6. See how close to the correct arrangement they came while you reveal the proper setting as shown in the illustration.

7. After having cleared the table invite the rest of the class, one at a time, to come up and arrange one place setting.

8. Finally ask the class to divide into groups of three. One student will play Tom, one student will play Aunt Polly and one student will portray Huck. Ask Tom to introduce Huck to Aunt Polly. Remind Tom that he must present the younger person to the older, for example:
    "Aunt Polly may I introduce you to my new friend Huckleberry?"
Remind Aunt Polly that she would respond by saying "hello" or "how do you do." Remind Huck that he should then respond with something like: "I am very pleased to meet you, ma'am."

DR. HUCK'S REMEDIES AND CURES

OBJECTIVES: 1.   To make the student aware of the folklore that lives within the story.

                   2.   To give the students an opportunity to explore creative writing.

MATERIALS: Paper and pencils.

PROCEDURE: 1.   Begin discussion on "folk remedies" by reading from the story the following two chants for getting rid of warts:

> Devil follow corpse
> cat follow devil
> warts follow cat
> I'm done with ye!

Remind the class that Huck had a definite set of directions as to where and when you had to speak this chant - in a graveyard at midnight when devils appear.

> Barley-corn, barley-corn,
> Injun meal shorts
> Spunk water, spunk
> water swaller these warts.

The directions with this chant demand that it take place in the middle of the woods at midnight next to a spunk water stump.

2.   Ask the class if they have ever heard any rhymes or chants that are designed to ward off sickness or bad luck. Discussion should follow.

3.   Divide the class into groups of four. Ask students to think of an illness or an event they would like to cure or prevent. Tell them that they are to collectively write a short chant to accomplish this. They are also to write a set of directions as to where, when and how the chant should be executed.

4.   Share the chants orally with the whole class by asking each group to perform it as a chorus.

TOM - A KNIGHT IN SHINING ARMOR

OBJECTIVES:
1. To make students aware of the friendship between Becky and Tom.

2. To call attention to the character traits of Becky Thatcher and Tom Sawyer.

3. To encourage students to focus on the facets of friendship.

MATERIALS: Paper, pencils (or if possible quill pens and ink).

PROCEDURE:
1. Brainstorm with students about the meaning of friendship with questions like, "What is a friend? How do you know when someone is your friend? Are friends important? When do you need friends the most?" The teacher may wish to write some of the students' ideas on the board.

2. Focusing upon *The Adventures of Tom Sawyer*, the teacher should try to elicit examples of true friendship exhibited so far in the book. The teacher should point out the relationship between Tom and Huck (which intensifies later), the relationship of the "pirates," and the intensifying relationship of Tom and Becky. The teacher may wish to relate qualities in these friendships to the list on the board.

3. One sign of true friendship in *The Adventures of Tom Sawyer* occurs when Tom takes Becky's punishment. Assign this episode to be read by the class.

4. Following the reading, ask all the girls to pretend they are Becky, and ask all the boys to pretend they are Tom. Tell your students that Tom has just taken Becky's punishment, and Becky must now slip him a note to thank him and express her appreciation. Tom must respond with a note.

5. Students can share these notes with the class.

WANTED

DEAD OR ALIVE

WANTED DEAD OR ALIVE

OBJECTIVES:

    1.   To develop an awareness of point of view and how this technique affects a story presentation.

    2.   To help students become aware of characterizations and their importance in a classic.

MATERIALS: Poster board, markers, crayons, construction paper.

PROCEDURE:

    1.   Ask two students to "stage" a minor disagreement (nonphysical) in front of the class. Try to make the situation look "real" to the other students. After the disagreement, ask the other observers what they saw. Gather many points of view.

    2.   Tell students that *The Adventures of Tom Sawyer* is written in the third person. This means that we all know the characters in the story through the author's eyes. We also see from the "disagreement" that everyone sees something different in the same event.

    3.   Call attention to Injun Joe as he is portrayed in the graveyard. Discuss his character with the class eliciting students' points of view with questions like, "Do you like Injun Joe? Why or why not? How does the author feel about him? How do you know? What do you think Injun Joe looks like? Did he have a good reason to seek revenge? Does the author want you to like Injun Joe?"

    4.   Once students' points of view have been established ask students to pretend they are a posse whose duty is to hunt Joe. They must make "wanted" signs to alert all of his dangerous nature.

    5.   Have students make the signs and display them in the classroom until Joe is captured.

IT'S A SMALL WORLD

OBJECTIVES:

1. To help students relate to the time frame in history in which the adventures occurred.

2. To help students understand the importance of the setting and mood in which the adventures take place.

3. To help students understand (Twain's) Tom Sawyer's ingenuity in creating escapades within a "small town" framework.

MATERIALS:

Cardboard, shoe boxes, paper scraps, material scraps, found materials, crayons, markers, twigs, Popsicle sticks for stick puppets, pictures of schoolrooms and homes of the early 1800's.

PROCEDURE:

1. *The Adventures of Tom Sawyer* takes place in a small pre-Civil War Southern town. The students need to be reminded either through pictures or discussion that this was a pretelevision, precar, preradio, and preplastic time. Discuss with students the ways in which Tom or any young boy might spend leisure time under these circumstances.

2. During these times, life centered around a small area with limited resources. The teacher should point out that Tom managed to find adventure everywhere.

3. As the students read the adventures, small groups of children should be asked to construct the "setting" for each adventure. Use the accompanying blueprint to construct an example of a shoe box set. Each shoe box could remain visible until the book is completed. Settings might include:

Tom's house	church	courtroom
schoolhouse	tannery	haunted house
graveyard	Jackson Island	cave

During construction, students should be reminded to keep "time - 1830" in mind, as well as the mood of each scene.

4. Each group could then make finger puppets to reenact the scene for the class within the shoe box setting.

TRUE AND FALSE QUESTIONNAIRE
TOM SAWYER

1. Injun Joe helped Tom Sawyer whitewash the fence.

2. The author of *Tom Sawyer* was Mark Twain.

3. Sid was Tom's best friend.

4. Tom Sawyer was in love with Amy Lawrence before he met Becky Thatcher.

5. Huck Finn convinced Tom that dead cats are good for curing the measles.

6. When Becky tears a page in the teacher's book, Huck Finn takes her punishment.

7. Tom loved school and never played hooky.

8. Muff Potter stabs Doctor Robinson.

9. Tom Sawyer shares his Pain Killer with his cat.

10. Huck Finn, Tom Sawyer and Joe Harper go to Jackson's Island to be pirates.

11. Tom Sawyer attends his own funeral.

12. Huck Finn saves the Widow Douglas from Injun Joe.

13. Tom and Becky were lost in the cave for three weeks.

14. Injun Joe is arrested at the end of the story.

15. Huck Finn is adopted by the Widow Douglas.

16. Tom starts a gang of robbers but won't let Huck Finn be in the gang because Huck has a girl friend.

17. When Tom collected things for "allowing" his friends to whitewash the fence, he got keys, kites, tadpoles, marbles and a brass doorknob.

18. Widow Douglas would not let Huck Finn "...gape, stretch nor scratch before folks."

19. Tom and Huck made up chants so they could impress Becky Thatcher.

20. Tom and Becky played "Pac-Man" at the amusement park on Jackson's Island.

(1) F (2) T (3) F (4) T (5) F (6) F (7) F (8) F (9) T (10) T (11) T (12) T (13) F (14) F (15) T (16) F (17) T (18) T (19) F (20) F

MARK TWAIN
1835-1910

BORN Samuel Clemens, Mark Twain, was born in 1835 in Florida, Missouri.

FAMILY Twain's father, John Clemens, was a judge of the highest integrity. His mother was strict and highly religious. Twain was one of six children.

CHILDHOOD Since his father had little business sense, the Clemens family had little money. This caused Twain to concentrate on manufacturing his own fun with a group of close friends. He lived much of the time on his uncle's farm. There he made a lasting friendship with a slave named Uncle Dan'l.

CONTRIBUTIONS Mark Twain was the first author from the United States to get world attention by writing, particularly in an American idiom. A short story by the name of "The Celebrated Jumping Frog of Calaveras County" won him his first fame. Huckleberry Finn and Tom Sawyer have become classic figures in American literature.

INTERESTING FACT The character of Aunt Polly in *Tom Sawyer* was fashioned after Mark Twain's own mother. A playmate by the name of Annie Laurie Hawkins was the model of Becky Thatcher.

EPITAPH OR FINAL THOUGHT Mark Twain was born in 1835 as Halley's Comet streaked across the sky. He always felt "they came in together and they must go out together." He died on April 12, 1910, one day after Halley's Comet again visited the sky.

HEIDI

JOHANNA SPYRI

SENSORY SEEK

OBJECTIVES:

1. To help students focus on their senses, and the role sensory experiences play in interpreting the environment.
2. To help students relate to Heidi's world.
3. To make students aware of details as they read.
4. To help students focus on Spyri's masterful use of description.

MATERIALS: Black bread, cheese, sausage (optional), tape recorder, pencil, paper, drawing paper, crayons.

PROCEDURE:

1. Spyri's unique talent for using description is evident throughout *Heidi*. The description is so vivid, our senses are stimulated almost totally throughout the story. In order to help students focus both on their senses and Spyri's use of description, the teacher may wish to use all, or a combination, of the following activities. After each activity, the teacher may wish to have students "search" for an example of Spyri's description in the book.

2. a. Gustatory: Teacher could share a snack of bread, cheese, milk and sausage (optional) with the class to demonstrate Heidi's mountain diet.

   b. Olefactory: Heidi was fascinated with the smell of mountain flowers. Season permitting, have students bring to class a variety of flowers. Allow students to smell and identify the flowers. Later, see if students can identify the flowers blindfolded, i.e., by odor only.

   c. Visual: The Alpine sunset was one of the most vivid descriptions in the book. Read a description to the class and ask students to illustrate the scene.

   d. Tactile: Heidi's mountain bed was made of hay covered with a "coarse piece of stuff." Students could take turns sitting on a burlap bag filled with straw or hay to identify with Heidi's sleeping "comfort." Or, Peter's grandmother was blind. In order to understand her circumstances, blindfolded students could be asked to identify everyday objects or classmates.

   e. Auditory: The wind howling through the fir trees was music to Heidi's ears. Students could make a tape of the howling wind, including branches breaking and birds chirping. Several groups could tape their interpretation of these sounds, and the tapes could be shared with the class.

GUESS WHAT'S COMING TO DINNER

OBJECTIVES:

    1.   To employ role playing in order to gain empathy with some of the story's main characters.

    2.   To experience the positive socialization process of creative drama.

MATERIALS:

A table, three chairs, some dinnerware, a tablecloth for the kittens to hide under, a tray for Sebastian, a shawl for Fraulein, bow ribbons for Clara and cloth bag.

PROCEDURE:

1.   Discuss the dinner table scene following Heidi's return from the tower with the kittens. Bring out the fact that Heidi is rushed into the dining room before she can dispose of the newly acquired kittens.

2.   Discuss the characters in this scene:

    a.   Fraulein Rottenmeir is a very proper and strict lady, who is furious at Heidi for leaving the house and being gone so long. She thinks Heidi is being disrespectful by answering her with "Meow."

    b.   Clara is a sweet girl who gets great enjoyment from all the exciting things Heidi causes to happen. She, however, does not understand why Heidi continues to make Fraulein Rottenmeir mad by answering with "Meows."

    c.   Heidi is worried that Fraulein Rottenmeir will discover the kittens. She tries to explain several times that she is not saying "meow," but the Fraulein just gets angrier and angrier.

    d.   Sebastian notices one of the kittens peeping out of Heidi's pocket as he is serving dinner. Consequently, as the scene progresses he finds it funnier and funnier and must leave the room for fear of laughing out loud at the predicament.

    e.   The kittens are playful and energetic. They will not stay hidden for long. (Hide the students who are playing the role of the kittens under the table and tablecloth.)

3.   Cast the scene. Remind the person portraying Fraulein Rottenmeir that she would sit up very properly at the table even though she is furious. Remind the student who plays Clara that although she is in a wheelchair, she greatly enjoys watching the activity. Remind the student who portrays Heidi that she is afraid that she is going to get in trouble. Furthermore, she is shifting around in her seat in order to try to keep the kittens hidden. Remind the student portraying Sebastian that he tries to be a proper servant, but he is about to lose control to laughter. Remind the students portraying the kittens that they meow more and more as the scene progresses. When they get free, however, they scatter all over the room in a playful manner. Play the scene when ready.

A MIND'S EYE VIEW OF ALM-UNCLE'S HUT

OBJECTIVES:
1. To encourage the process of acquiring a mental picture from literary description.

2. To gain an understanding of Johanna Spyri's descriptive style.

MATERIALS:
Descriptive passage dealing with the inside of Alm-Uncle's hut, drawing paper, pencils and markers.

PROCEDURE:
1. Explain to the class that the descriptive style in literature is merely a style that draws mental images in the reader's mind. Although each reader's mental picture of the same description will be slightly different, basically the mental pictures will have much in common. In other words, "a large kettle" may be one color and shape in one reader's mental picture and another color and shape in another reader's mental picture. Nevertheless, both mental pictures will contain "a large kettle." The differences are due to the fact that each reader draws on his own experience with large kettles to fill in the color and shape.

2. Read Spyri's descriptive passage of the inside of Alm-Uncle's hut to the class. Ask the students to close their eyes and paint a mental picture of the inside of Alm-Uncle's hut as you supply them with details.

3. Ask the students to see in their mind's eye the size of the room, the table and chair, the grandfather's bed off in one corner and the large door and cupboards where clothes were hung. Ask them to concentrate also on the plates, cups, glasses, bread, smoked meat and cheese.

4. Pass out copies of the descriptive passage to each student along with drawing paper and markers. Ask each student to draw a picture of the inside of Alm-Uncle's hut from the descriptive paragraph.

5. Display all the pictures so that the class can see how each individual interpreted the same descriptive passage.

6. If there is a picture of this scene in the text, read to the class, make sure the class does not see it before each student has an opportunity to draw a version.

WHEELCHAIR VIEW

OBJECTIVES: 1.   To help children understand the meaning and ramifications of various types of handicaps.

                2.   To help children focus on the characterizations of Heidi, Grandpa, Clara, and Peter's grandmother.

                3.   To give students an opportunity to role play.

MATERIALS: Dictionary and wheelchair (optional).

PROCEDURE: 1.   Ask students to use a dictionary to locate a definition of "handicapped." Within the definition, students will find reference to a disadvantage. Discuss each of the following characters with students to see if students can recognize the "handicap" in each:

    a.   Clara: physically handicapped - inability to walk.
    b.   Grandmother (Peter's) physically handicapped - inability to see.
    c.   Grandfather - socially handicapped - refusal to communicate.
    d.   Some students might even be able to recognize that Peter is somewhat handicapped because of his financial situation and inability to communicate his thoughts directly.

                2.   Discuss the ramifications of a "handicap" with students with questions like: "What disadvantages do handicapped people have? Advantages? How do people in the story overcome their handicaps? Do the people in the story compensate in any way? How should handicapped people be helped? How would you have helped Clara? Grandmother? Peter? etc."

                3.   To help students understand the "bond" between Clara and Heidi, or male counterparts, teacher may wish to divide students into pairs. One student in the pair would play the role of Clara, or a physically handicapped person, and one student could play the role of Heidi, the companion. During one recess, "Heidi" would be assigned to entertain "Clara" (i.e., read to her, sit with her, bring her school supplies, etc.) while the other children are all outside having fun. If a wheelchair is available, it might be used for this activity. During the next recess, students could "switch" roles.

                4.   When all students have had a turn to play both roles, reactions from both points of view could be discussed.

HELP WANTED

• • • • • •

COMPANION FOR CLARA

Duties of Position:

Skills Required:

Working Conditions:

Salary:
Educational Background:

Preferred Age Range:
Personality Characteristics:

HELP WANTED - A COMPANION FOR CLARA

OBJECTIVES: 1.   To gain an understanding of point of view.

2.   To experience expository writing.

MATERIALS: Copies of the Help Wanted ad form as found on the illustration page and pencils

PROCEDURE: 1.   Discuss with the class the disappointment Fraulein Rottenmeir expresses with Heidi as a suitable companion for Clara.

a.   Heidi's name did not please her. It was not a proper name but rather a nickname.

b.   Heidi's appearance did not please her. Her plain cotton dress and old crushed straw hat was not fine.

c.   Heidi's age did not please her. She was a full four years younger than twelve-year-old Clara.

d.   Heidi's educational background did not please her. She could not even read!

2.   Ask the class members to write a help wanted ad for a companion for Clara from Fraulein Rottenmeir's strict and proper point of view. Include physical characteristics, what hobbies this companion should have, what likes and dislikes she should have and what her duties would be.

3.   Next, ask the class members to write a help wanted ad for a companion for Clara from Clara's point of view. Her thoughts would be very different from those of Fraulein Rottenmeir. Remind the students to keep in mind the needs of a child locked into a wheelchair.

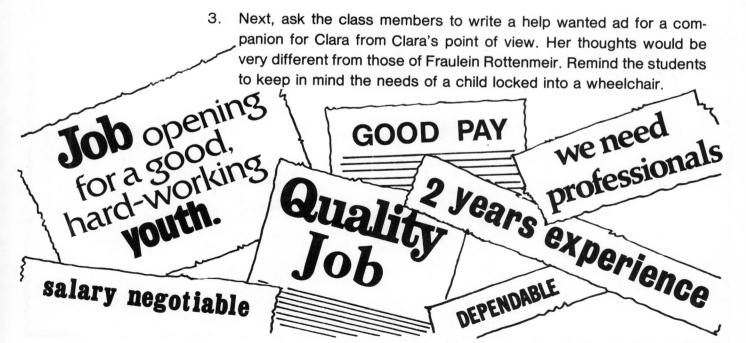

WHY PETER CAN'T READ

OBJECTIVES:
1. To help students understand the character of Peter.
2. To help students understand Peter's difficulties with learning to read.
3. To help students relate to various methods in learning and teaching people to read.
4. To reinforce knowledge of parts of speech.

MATERIALS: Paper, pencil, tape recorder (optional).

PROCEDURE:

1. Throughout *Heidi*, Peter was a very hesitant learner. He created a variety of excuses for not attending school. Discuss these excuses with the class. Toward the end of the story, the reader discovers that even the schoolmaster has given up on Peter's ability to read. Ask students to help you locate this passage in the story.

2. Heidi helps Peter learn to read by reciting the poem (within the story text) with the young shepherd. Ask students to relate to their own experiences about learning to read by asking questions like: "Do you remember when you learned to read? Who taught you? How were you taught? How did you feel? Is reading important? Why?"

3. Once Peter began to read, especially when he was reading to his grandmother, he made it a habit of omitting words he didn't know. To allow students to "experience" his habit, ask students, one at a time to orally read the ABC poem in the book. However, during this reading, students should be asked to leave out certain words. For example, one student could read the poem leaving out all the nouns. Another might leave out all the verbs, etc.

4. These presentations can be tape-recorded, and then discussed. "What happens when you skip words? Why was Peter's grandmother uncomfortable when he read? etc."

TRUE AND FALSE QUESTIONNAIRE
HEIDI

1. Heidi preferred to live in the city rather than to remain at Alm-Uncle's hut.

2. Heidi's grandfather destroyed Clara's wheelchair so that Clara could never leave his house.

3. Dete, Heidi's sister, was the person who introduced the child to her grandfather.

4. Heidi's grandfather was well-known and everyone loved him.

5. Sebastian thought it was very humorous when Heidi tried to smuggle the cats into Clara's house.

6. Johanna Spyri was the author of *Heidi*.

7. Heidi spent many hours helping Peter learn to read.

8. Peter's grandmother helped him herd the sheep every day.

9. Grandfather's goats were named Little Swan and Little Bear.

10. Fraulein Rottenmeir loved pets and was thrilled when she saw the baby kittens.

11. Although she loved Clara very much, Heidi missed her grandfather and Peter while she lived with Clara.

12. Heidi's allergies bothered her when she was near the mountain flowers, so she went to live with Clara.

13. Heidi's grandfather never went to church because he didn't have a car.

14. When Peter read to his grandmother, he often skipped words that he couldn't pronounce.

15. Heidi loved books and wanted to learn to read after she met Clara's grandmother.

16. Heidi always shared her dinner with Peter when they went to the mountains with the goats.

17. As a reward for helping Clara, Mr. Sesemann left Peter $1.00 per week for the rest of his life.

18. During the winter, Alm-Uncle took Heidi to visit Peter's grandmother in a sled.

19. Heidi saved candy to take home to Peter's grandmother. She kept the candy in her wardrobe at Clara's house.

(1) F (2) F (3) T (4) F (5) T (6) T (7) T (8) F (9) T (10) F (11) T (12) F (13) F (14) T (15) T (16) T (17) F (18) T (19) F

JOHANNA SPYRI
1827 - 1901

BORN Johanna Spyri was born on July 12, 1827, in Hirzel, Switzerland, near Zurich.

FAMILY Johanna Spyri's father was Johann Jacob Heusser. He was a doctor. Her mother, Meta, was a poet and songwriter. Johanna was the fourth child in a family of six children.

CHILDHOOD As a child Johanna loved books and attended a small village school for a short while. Her home was a happy one populated by two brothers, Theodor and Christian, and three sisters, Netti, Ega and Meta. Her grandparents, her tutor and the tutor's children all lived under one roof. As a child she wrote verses.

CONTRIBUTIONS *Heidi* has been read and loved by generations of children. In 1937 a film was made of the book starring Shirley Temple and Jean Hersholt. Another popular book by Johanna Spyri was *Jorli: The Story of a Swiss Boy.*

INTERESTING FACT Johanna Spyri married Bernhard Spyri when she was twenty-five. They had one son who died of tuberculosis. Johanna did not begin her formal writing career until she was forty-three years old!

EPITAPH OR FINAL THOUGHTS Johanna died on July 7, 1901. Her books are characterized by the child's point of view. She shows children as those who suffer, too. This suffering was first know to Johanna when her grandmother, Anna Schweizer Gessner, died.

THE WIZARD OF OZ

L. FRANK BAUM

FOLLOW THE YELLOW BRICK ROAD

OBJECTIVES:

    1.   To explore the main characters in order to understand how their inner feelings influence the way they talk, walk, and relate to their environment.

    2.   To experience creative movement.

MATERIALS:

Rolls of yellow crepe paper, the record from the sound track of the film *The Wizard of Oz* and a cleared area.

PROCEDURE:

    1.   Divide the class into groups of five. Ask each group to decide who in that group will portray what characters - Toto, Lion, Scarecrow, Dorothy, and the Tin Woodman.

    2.   Ask everyone portraying Toto to remember that he is a relatively small dog, for Dorothy easily held him in her arms; he is very quick in movement and probably has a high-pitched bark.

    3.   Ask everyone portraying Dorothy to remember that she is the leader of the group, very spirited and happy, yet determined. She may hum along with the record as she walks.

    4.   Ask everyone portraying the Lion to remember that he is probably very slow moving and afraid; he walks slightly slouched due to his lack of courage, and he is a very large animal. He may cry now and then as things frighten him.

    5.   Ask everyone portraying the Scarecrow to remember his movements are uncontrollable; his arms, legs, neck and head are limp like a rag doll.

    6.   Ask everyone portraying the Tin Woodman to remember that he walks stiff-legged like a toy soldier, his head, neck and arms are straight and rigid. He is probably not very happy because he has no heart.

    7.   Next, have the students move around the room the way the characters portrayed would move - practice.

    8.   Ask for volunteers to take the yellow crepe paper and wind two ribbons of color representing the sides of the road, around the room.

    9.   Play the music from the film track and allow one group of five friends at a time to walk, skip and dance down the yellow brick road together. When one group has followed the road to the end, let the next group begin.

DESTINATION OZ

OBJECTIVES:
1. To encourage students to think about the characterization of Dorothy.
2. To stimulate students' imagination.
3. To help students review the various settings in *The Wizard of Oz*.
4. To encourage students to think of creative uses for everyday objects.
5. To offer experiences in creating problem solving.

MATERIALS:
Suitcase, materials "found" in either the classroom or at home.

PROCEDURE:
1. At the beginning of the story, Baum indicates that Toto is Dorothy's **only** playmate. She lived in a little farmhouse with one room. Research indicates that people whose childhood was limited in either peer relationships or material things tend to become "creative" in fashioning activities in order to keep busy. Dorothy might be thought about in these terms. She "created" an entire world in which to function. She created playmates, challenges, and fantasy.

2. Ask students to pretend they are "like" Dorothy or a male counterpart. Students should be divided into groups of three or four. Each group should be assigned to walk into one part of Dorothy's world. Groups could be assigned to places like:

Munchkin Land	Land of Winged Monkeys
Cornfield	Kansas City
Great Forest	Land of Quadlings
Emerald City	Hammer-Head Hill

3. Students should be told that they are to "plan" a trip to their assigned land. Unlike Dorothy, they know the place they will visit, and can take three things that fit in a suitcase, to help them either survive or better enjoy their land. Allow students to bring things from home. For example, students may wish to take a book to Kansas City to prevent boredom. They may wish to bring rags to the cornfield to help stuff the scarecrow, etc. Students may wish to use things in a creative fashion. For example, bring a hanger to the forest to use as a bow to shoot the witch.

4. Once groups have gathered their materials, they should place them in a suitcase and orally present their "survival packs" to the class, discussing reasons for their selections.

DEAR DOROTHY

OBJECTIVES:

1. To help students become aware of the various settings in the Land of Oz.

2. To help students better understand the three major characters who live in the Land of Oz.

3. To encourage students to reflect upon the consequences of achieving a goal.

MATERIALS: Postcard-size paper, pencils, crayons, markers.

PROCEDURE:

1. At the end of the story, everyone's wishes are fulfilled. The Lion has his courage, the Scarecrow has his brain, and the Tin Woodman has his heart. Dorothy returns to Kansas. Each character is assigned a "happily-ever-after environment" in which to reside. The Scarecrow is to rule the Emerald City. The Tin Woodman will be King of the Winkies, and the Lion can be King of the Beasts.

2. Ask students to reflect upon having achieved a goal with questions like: "Have you ever wanted anything very badly? Did you get it? How? What happened after you got it? Do you still treasure it? Will you always treasure it? Ask students to think about the Lion, Scarecrow and Tin Woodman. How do you think they feel about their "wishes" now?

3. Divide students into three groups, a Lion group, a Tin Woodman group and a Scarecrow group. Either individually or in groups, have students "become" these characters, and write postcards to Dorothy telling her:
   a. How they are using their new treasures.
   b. What life is like in their new environments.
   c. How life is different.

4. Have students then illustrate their picture postcards to show their new environments - i.e., Lion in Woods, Tin Woodman as King of Winkies, and Scarecrow as ruler of Emerald City.

DOROTHY'S OLD-FASHIONED TRIVIA BEE

OBJECTIVES: 1.   To encourage careful reading.

2.   To encourage recall of literary details.

MATERIALS: Question-and-answer sheets, Tin Woodman's heart as the prize.

PROCEDURE: 1.   Have the class ring the room in spelling bee style.

2.   Using the thirty questions, conduct a trivia bee to see who will win the Tin Woodman's heart. (see illustration page)

Trivia Questions

1. How did the Wicked Witch of the East die?
2. What were the magic words used to call forth the Winged Monkeys?
3. In what state did Dorothy live?
4. In what visual form did Oz first appear to Dorothy?
5. Who saw Oz as a fierce beast?
6. What did the Good Witch give Dorothy that protected her?
7. How does the Wicked Witch first try to get rid of Dorothy and her friends?
8. Who saves the Scarecrow from drowning?
9. What color did the Quadlings like to wear and use for house paint?
10. Who captures Dorothy and takes her to the Wicked Witch of the West?
11. Who gave the green spectacles to Dorothy and her friends?
12. How did Oz first appear visually to the Lion?
13. What was Uncle Henry doing when Dorothy returned from Oz?
14. With what did the Wizard make the Scarecrow's brain?
15. Who was Dorothy's only playmate in Kansas?
16. Who wrote *The Wizard of Oz*?
17. Where did the Scarecrow go after the adventure was complete?
18. What caused Dorothy to get caught in the cyclone?
19. What was the Good Witch's first name?
20. Where did the Wizard work prior to coming to Oz?

21. What did Dorothy have to do to the shoes in order to get back to Kansas?

22. What color were the magic shoes?

23. Who did the Wicked Witch of the West make her slaves?

24. Where did the Lion go after the adventure was completed?

25. Where did the Hammer-Heads live?

26. What monster did the Lion have to kill in order to be King of the Beasts?

27. What did the Tin Woodman do to cause Dorothy to first notice him?

28. What did the Scarecrow think was the most valuable thing in the world?

29. Where was Oz headed as he departed in a balloon?

30. What group in the story had to obey the Golden Cap?

ANSWER SHEET

1. Dorothy's house fell on her.
2. ZIZ-ZY, ZVZ-ZY, ZIK!
3. Kansas
4. A talking head
5. The Tin Woodman
6. A kiss
7. She sends a pack of wolves
8. The Stork
9. Red
10. The Winged Monkeys
11. The Guardian of the Gates
12. A ball of fire
13. Milking a cow
14. Bran, needles and pins
15. Toto
16. L. Frank Baum
17. To rule the Emerald City
18. She went to rescue Toto who was frightened
19. Glinda
20. Circus
21. Click the heels three times
22. Silver
23. Winkies
24. To the forest as King of the Beasts
25. On a hill
26. A giant spider
27. Groan
28. Brains
29. Omaha
30. Winged Monkeys

SOUND TRAVELLER

OBJECTIVES:

1. To help students focus upon the ongoing contrast between reality and fantasy in *The Wizard of Oz*.

2. To develop auditory awareness in students.

3. To encourage students to use their imagination.

MATERIALS:

Anything "found" in the classroom environment, tape recorder. Optional: strip of tinfoil, whistles, birdcalls, bells.

PROCEDURE:

1. In order to take Dorothy from her "real" world in Kansas to the fanciful world of Oz, Baum creates a cyclone which sweeps Dorothy and Toto away. This transition is a key factor in Baum's ability to combine fantasy and reality.

2. To demonstrate this contrast, divide students into groups of eight. One group will be a "cyclone," one will be the Land of Oz. (This activity can be repeated so everyone has a turn.) Ask each group to talk about the sounds they could hear in their assigned environment.
   a. The cyclone would include wind, shutters banging, girl screaming, dog barking, thunder, rain, etc.
   b. Oz would include birds singing, Munchkin sounds, crickets chirping, gentle breezes, etc.

3. Each person in the group can decide which sound to be. One student begins making his sound, and other sounds are added cumulatively. (The lightest sound should go first.)

4. Rehearse, then tape-record.

5. Tapes, when replayed, should emphasize the difference between the loud cyclone and the sweet sounds of Oz.

A FUNNY THING HAPPENED
ON THE WAY TO EMERALD CITY

OBJECTIVES:

1. To demonstrate the unifying role that the yellow brick road plays in the story.

2. To reinforce the plot sequence.

3. To experience socialization via the participation of the entire class in mural making.

4. To enjoy a visual art experience.

MATERIALS: A roll of butcher paper and magic markers.

PROCEDURE:

1. Discuss the function of the yellow brick road as it relates to the story. Note that most of the action takes place either on the road or in a spot arrived at via the road.

2. Attach the butcher paper to the wall and run it around the room in mural fashion. Draw a yellow brick road all the way around it.

3. Ask students to divide themselves in pairs to draw various scenes from the story in the appropriate sequence on the yellow brick road. Depending on the version read by the class, the basic plot sequence could be ordered as follows:

   a. Dorothy and Toto play on the prairie in Kansas.
   b. The sky darkens as the cyclone hits. The house swirls up into the the eye of the storm.
   c. Dorothy's house lands on the Wicked Witch of the East. The Munchkins meet Dorothy.
   d. Dorothy makes friends with the Scarecrow.
   e. Dorothy makes friends with the Tin Woodman.
   f. Dorothy meets the Cowardly Lion.
   g. Taking a trip to Oz through the poppy field.
   h. Entering the Emerald City.
   i. Talking to the Great Oz.
   j. Conquering the Wicked Witch
   k. All wishes are granted.
   l. Glinda helps Dorothy return home.

TRUE AND FALSE QUESTIONNAIRE
WIZARD OF OZ

1. Before Dorothy visited the Land of Oz, she lived in New York City.

2. The Tin Woodman was afraid of rain; the Scarecrow was afraid of fire; and the Lion was afraid of everything.

3. Toto always obeyed Dorothy.

4. The Quadlings were lobsters who did a square dance.

5. Dorothy was swept into Oz by a violent tornado.

6. At the end of the story, the Tin Woodman became King of the Winkies.

7. L. Frank Baum was the author of *The Wizard of Oz.*

8. The Wizard was going to take everyone home in his spaceship.

9. The Winged Monkeys had to obey the Golden Cap.

10. The Hammer-Heads lived in Kansas City.

11. The yellow brick road was the street that took Dorothy to the Emerald City.

12. The first friend Dorothy and Toto made in Oz was the Cowardly Lion.

13. Glinda was a good witch.

14. The Guardian of the Gate gave Dorothy the green spectacles.

15. Glinda had a crystal ball through which she watched Dorothy and her friends.

16. Dorothy really missed Aunt Em and Uncle Henry while she was in Oz.

17. The whole time she was in Oz, Dorothy knew she was just dreaming.

18. The Munchkins were servants of the Wicked Witch of the West.

19. The magic slippers allowed Dorothy to fly anywhere in Oz.

20. The Tin Woodman wanted a heart.

21. The Lion had to kill a giant spider.

22. The Winged Monkeys became Dorothy's friends and killed the Wicked Witch for Dorothy.

(1) F (2) T (3) F (4) F (5) F (6) T (7) T (8) F (9) T (10) F (11) T (12) F (13) T (14) T (15) F (16) T (17) F (18) F (19) F (20) T (21) T (22) F

L. FRANK BAUM
1856 - 1919

BORN Lyman Frank Baum was born on May 15, 1856, in Chittenango, New York.

FAMILY L. Frank Baum was the son of Benjamin Ward Baum, an oil dealer, and Cynthia Stanton. He was the seventh child to be born to the family.

CHILDHOOD He had a comfortable childhood in a mansion north of Syracuse, New York, called Rose Lawn. He also had an inventive childhood characterized by such activity as putting out an amateur newspaper with his younger brother Harry. The newspaper which lasted three years was called *The Rose Lawn Home Journal.* His sister Harriet continually encouraged him to write.

CONTRIBUTIONS L. Frank Baum wrote many stories for children during his lifetime. *The Wizard of Oz* won him the Lewis Carroll Award in 1968. He often wrote under pseudonyms such as Captain Hugh Fitzgerald, Schuyler Staunton and Floyd Ahers.

INTERESTING FACT *The Wizard of Oz* was titled after the third drawer of Baum's filing cabinet. The first drawer was marked A - G, the second drawer was H - N and the third was O - Z.

EPITAPH OR FINAL THOUGHTS Frank Baum died in 1919. He had always felt that the Great Writer (God) had written *The Wizard of Oz*, using him only as an instrument. The whole story came to him in a flash. In fact, since he didn't even have time to find the proper writing paper, he wrote it on old envelopes.

ALICE IN WONDERLAND AND THROUGH THE LOOKING GLASS

LEWIS CARROLL

THE UNBIRTHDAY TEA PARTY

OBJECTIVES:
1. To gain an understanding of the character of Alice.
2. To experience some of Carroll's fancies such as an unbirthday, a game of croquet and an English tea party.
3. To exercise the imagination.

MATERIALS:
Teacups and saucers, tea, comfits (candy filled with nuts or fruits), biscuits or scones, treacle (mild molasses) or jams, currants, plum cake (optional), croquet set, napkins, an unbirthday present brought from home by each student and a space to play.

PROCEDURE:
1. Discuss with the class the concept of the unbirthday party put forth by Humpty Dumpty. Why did he think it was a good idea?
2. Tell the students that they have been invited to Alice's Unbirthday Party. Ask them to consider what gift they could bring for her from home. In doing this ask them to go through the story and write down all the facts that they can about Alice, her likes and dislikes. For instance, what would be appropriate for Alice?

She is 7½ years old.	She is English.
She is fond of social games.	She likes school.
She is very curious.	She is polite.
She is very smart.	She likes cats.
She does not like to play games when there are no rules.	She does not like ill-mannered people.

3. The day of the party, ask each guest to show the gift and tell why it would be appropriate as an unbirthday present for Alice.
4. After the gifts have been revealed, ask the class to play a game of conventional croquet. Ask the participants to imagine how difficult it would be to play if their mallets were live flamingos and their balls were hedgehogs.
5. The final activity would consist of experiencing an English tea party. Encourage students to notice how less sweet English biscuits, scones or cakes taste than what they are used to, how very much like raisins are the currants and how many flavors there are of jams and marmalades.
6. The class may want to sing "Happy Unbirthday to You" before tasting the plum cake.

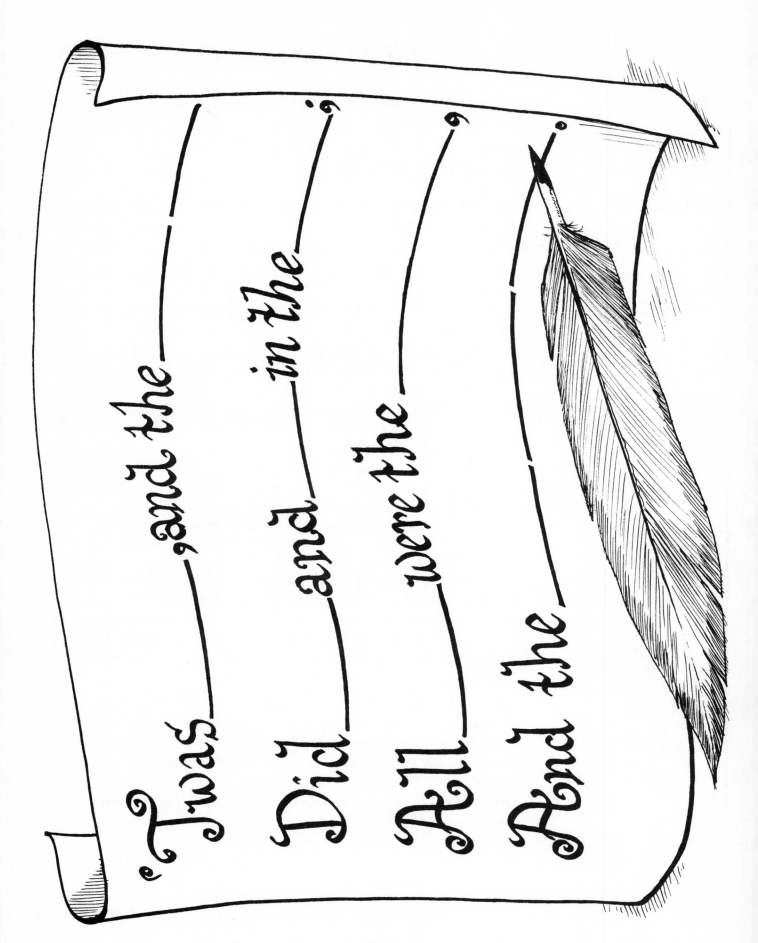

'Twas _____ ,and the

Did _____ and _____ in the

All _____ were the

And the _____

48

LOOKING GLASS POETRY

OBJECTIVES:
1. To experience the joy of nonsense poetry.
2. To exercise visual awareness.

MATERIALS:
A large mirror, pencils and papers.

PROCEDURE:
1. Read "Jabberwocky" to the class. Explain that it is an example of nonsense poetry. In other words, many of the words are made up and cannot be found in a dictionary.

2. Discuss Humpty Dumpty's definition of the following nonsense words. Note how the words sound like their definitions and how some are made up of a combination of two other words.

brillig	(broiling time)
slithy	(lithe and slimy)
tories	(something like badgers, lizards and corkscrews)
gyre	(go round)
gimble	(to make holes)
wahe	(grass plot round a sundial)
mimsy	(flimsy and miserable)
borogoues	(thin shabby bird)
mome	(green pig)
raths	(from home)
outgrabe	(bellowing and whistling)

3. Ask the students to organize themselves into pairs. Each pair must write a nonsense poem based on the "Jabberwocky" structure by filling in the blanks. Remind the students to create words that sound like the definitions they have in mind. Pass out copies of illustration page.

   'Twas _____, and the _____ _____
   Did _____ and _____ in the _____;
   All _____ were the _____,
   And the _____ _____ _____.

4. After the poems have been created and every nonsense word has a definition, ask the students to copy them **backwards** on a large sheet of paper. Please print. Remind the students to make both the letters and the sequence of letters backwards.

5. Students will share their looking glass poems by holding them up in front of the mirror for the rest of the class to read.

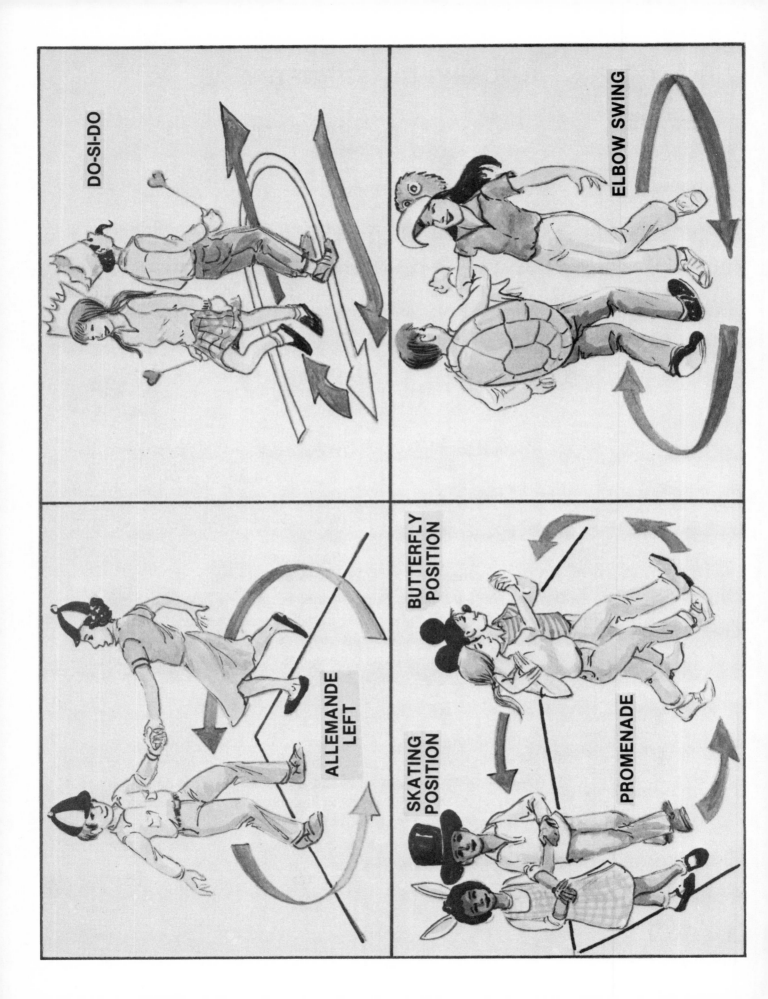

LEWIS CARROLL'S QUADRILLE

OBJECTIVES:
1. To exercise the imagination in relation to body and space.

2. To experience the joy of creative movement.

3. To experience teamwork.

MATERIALS: Space for square dancing.

PROCEDURE:
1. Discuss the Lobster's Quadrille which the Mock Turtle and the Gryphon described to Alice. Emphasize that, as in all the games Alice encounters, the dance starts out sounding like a lovely square dance but soon becomes confused beyond recognition. Lobsters are thrown into the sea, the dancers swim after them and turn somersaults in the water.

2. Incorporating a few square dance techniques such as allemande left, allemande right, promenades, do-si-dos (described on the illustration page), ask each group of nine to create their own quadrille (square dance) in honor of Lewis Carroll. Eight dancers should be paired off so that four pairs of partners occupy the square. The ninth member of the group would be the "caller" of the dance.

3. Encourage the groups to write the various movements down as they create. Include claps, jumps, kicks, hops and turns. Perhaps more imaginative movement would be generated if each person assumed a character's role from the stories. For instance, one pair of partners could be the March Hare and the Mad Hatter. The second pair could be the King and the Queen of Hearts. The third could be Tweedledum and Tweedledee; and the fourth could be Alice and the Dormouse.

4. When the dance has been created on paper, ask the group to try it out on the floor. The caller can read from the notes. Encourage the caller to speak the directions with rhythm in his/her voice.

5. Each group should demonstrate its Carroll Quadrille.

6. This demonstration could be set to music, video-taped or presented to another class.

7. The teacher may wish to have a dance contest with the Lobster, played by a student, and the Turtle, played by a student, acting as judges.

THE DAY THE TARTS DISAPPEARED

OBJECTIVES:

1. To help students relate to the absurdity of the famous "Who Stole the Tart" trial in *Alice in Wonderland*.

2. To introduce students to some courtroom procedure and terminology.

3. To give students experience in story playing.

MATERIALS:

These materials are optional; any or all can be used: judge-like wig, crown, slates and pencils for jurors, rabbit ears, mouse ears, scroll, trumpet, hat, teacup, bread, spectacles, large canvas bag, pepper box, poster boards with symbols (diamonds, clubs, hearts, spades) on each.

PROCEDURE:

1. To help students appreciate the famous trial scene (a dramatic reenactment of the scene is a helpful technique). Arrange chairs in classroom in courtroom style so there are two for the King and Queen, twelve chairs in a jury box, and one chair for a witness stand. All other chairs should be arranged in rows to represent a courtroom. The King, of course, is the judge wearing a "great wig" with a crown on top.

2. The jury box should be filled with students "role playing" a variety of beasts and birds. Be sure to include a lizard and a guinea pig. Each student should select a role to play (frog, squirrel, duck, etc.), and each animal should have a slate to keep notes during the trial. The "animals" may wish to use other props like ears, hats, tails, etc.

3. Alice could enter the courtroom and the trial could begin using the dialogue as it is written in the chapters entitled "Who Stole the Tarts?" and "Alice's Evidence." All students can partake, as the courtroom is filled, and students could switch roles.

4. The scene should be fast-moving, and students may need to be reminded to stay in character at all times.

5. Recap scene as follows:
   a. Everyone including Alice is seated. Knave is chained and guarded. Rabbit waits with trumpet and scroll in hands while Alice speaks to Gryphon about "stupid things."
   b. Trumpet blasts - accusation read.
   c. Trumpet blasts - first witness called.
   d. Hatter, March Hare, Dormouse enter.
   e. The three have dialogue with King and Queen.

f.   Alice begins to grow.

g.   Dormouse reacts.

h.   Guinea Pig cheers and is stuffed into canvas bag.

i.   Trumpet blasts - next witness called.

j.   Duchess' cook enters with pepper. Everyone in courtroom sneezes.

k.   Cook has dialogue with King and Queen.

l.   Trumpet blasts - Alice is next witness.

m.   Alice, King and Queen have dialogue about size.

n.   White Rabbit interrupts with the "White Paper" evidence.

o.   White Rabbit reads evidence in court (he wears spectacles for this).

p.   Discussion about the "pun" ensues.

q.   Scene ends as Alice throws a deck of cards into the air during her discussion with the Queen.

6.   Once students have had an opportunity to practice the scene, if the facilities are available, the scene could be video-taped. Scene could also be replayed with students switching roles.

PUNS ARE GOOD FOR BREAKFAST

OBJECTIVES:
1. To introduce students to puns and homonyms and show how these literary devices are used in *Alice in Wonderland.*
2. To give students experiences in using puns and homonyms.
3. To encourage creative thinking.

MATERIALS:
Paper, pencil, drawing paper, two bulletin boards if available.

PROCEDURE:
1. Discuss both puns and homonyms with students. A homonym is a set of words that sound alike, but are spelled differently, and mean different things. Words like here, hear; to, too, two; red, read; through, threw, etc., are homonyms. A pun, according to Webster, is "a humorous use of a word in such a way as to suggest different meanings or applications or of words having the same or nearly the same sound but different meanings." Puns are used quite often in commercials and advertisements to attract people's attention and make the ads humorous. Lewis Carroll was a master of the pun. Some examples of puns he used include:

   porpoise for purpose (Lobster Quadrille)
   soles and eels for soles and heels (Lobster Quadrille)
   a flower's face has "sense" in it (Live Flowers)
   a tree has a bark-bough-wough (Live Flowers)
   "Reeling and Writhing" for reading and writing (Mock Turtle's Story)
   "Ambition, Distraction, Uglification and Derision" for Addition, Subtraction, Multiplication and Division (Mock Turtle's Story)
   Tortoise for taught us (Mock Turtle's Story)

   Examples of homonyms in *Alice in Wonderland* include:
   flower - flour (Queen Alice)
   lesson - lessen (Mock Turtle)
   tail - tale (Caucus Race)
   knot - not (Caucus Race)

2. You may ask students to locate these "devices" in the books so students can see how Carroll "plays" with words. Discussion about what makes each example amusing could follow.

3. Ask students to try to make up some puns of their own. The teacher could list these on the board. Remind students to listen for word plays on TV and radio.

RULES, RULES, WHO MAKES THE RULES?

OBJECTIVES:
1. To help students understand the importance of games and rules in the works of Lewis Carroll.
2. To help students understand the importance of rules in their own lives.
3. To help students relate to the "wonder" in Carroll's works.

MATERIALS:
A variety of games, either board games or card games that the students are not familiar with.

PROCEDURE:
1. Remove all directions and rules from the game you have. Divide students into groups of four or five. Give each group one game that students are not familiar with and give only one direction to the class. Tell them to "play." Do not answer any questions about the games, and try not to help solve problems groups might be experiencing. Expect arguments and disagreements within the groups. Allow students to work with the games for about 15-20 minutes.
2. At the end of that time, hold a class discussion with questions like "What did you do? Did you have any problems? Why? Did you get along? Did you have fun playing the game? Could you have had more fun? How?"
3. Indicate to students that much of the "wonder" in *Alice in Wonderland* occurred because people played without rules. For example, Alice couldn't play croquet because the Queen kept changing the rules. This lack of a common set of guidelines made Alice as frustrated as people in the room were when they were asked to "play" without rules. If the teacher wishes, this discussion might be extended to social situations, government, etc.

56

TRUE AND FALSE QUESTIONNAIRE
ALICE IN WONDERLAND

1. Alice took a train ride to Wonderland.

2. Both *Alice in Wonderland* and *Through the Looking Glass* were written by Lewis Carroll.

3. Throughout the story, Alice's size kept changing because certain foods and drinks made her shrink and stretch.

4. Alice is a ten-year-old girl who had a pet dog named Toto.

5. In Wonderland, croquet was a game played using lobsters as mallets and live flamingos as balls.

6. Humpty Dumpty used nonsense words in the poem entitled "Jabberwocky."

7. Tweedledee had the word "Dee" embroidered on his collar.

8. The Duchess's cook made people sneeze because she carried a pepperbox with her.

9. Alice's sister dreamt about the adventures in *Through the Looking Glass*.

10. Alice met a group of animals called Puns and Homonyms who spent their time writing dictionaries.

11. Alice loved to play games without rules because she could be creative.

12. Dinah was Alice's cat.

13. The "Lobster's Quadrille" is another way of saying the "Lobster's Claw."

14. The White Rabbit was very concerned about keeping the Duchess waiting and he carried a pocket watch.

15. "Off with his/her head" was an expression the Queen used often.

16. Alice is called as a witness in the "Who Stole the Tarts" trial.

17. Alice was a poor student in school, and liked to daydream a lot.

18. Humpty Dumpty liked unbirthday presents because he could get 364 presents in one year.

19. Alice was impolite to everyone she met.

(1) F (2) T (3) T (4) F (5) F (6) T (7) T (8) T (9) T (10) F (11) F (12) T (13) F (14) T (15) T (16) T (17) F (18) T (19) F

LEWIS CARROLL
1832 - 1889

BORN Charles Lutwidge Dodgson, Lewis Carroll, was born on July 11, 1832, in the agricultural community of Cheshire in England.

FAMILY Carroll's father, the Reverend Charles Dodgson, was a scholar in both mathematics and the classics. He wanted his son to follow in his footsteps. Consequently, Lewis Carroll did become a lecturer in mathematics and a deacon of the church. His mother was Fanny Lutwidge. She had eleven children. Lewis Carroll was the oldest son.

CHILDHOOD As a child Carroll enjoyed working with his hands. In fact, he built a perfectly crafted miniature tool kit for his sister Elizabeth. He also liked to dress up as a magician and entertain his sister with magic tricks. The whole family rose early and worked late into the evening. Furthermore, they walked to church twice every Sunday.

CONTRIBUTIONS During his lifetime Carroll published ten books on mathematics and logic in addition to his beloved stories about Alice.

INTERESTING FACT In the summer of 1862, Carroll was telling a story to three little girls at a picnic. They were so delighted that they begged him to write it down. This story later became the basis of *Alice's Adventures Underground.*

EPITAPH OR FINAL THOUGHTS Death is over now; there is not that experience to be faced again.

THE
MERRY ADVENTURES
OF
ROBIN HOOD

HOWARD PYLE

ROBIN HOOD DAY

OBJECTIVES:
1. To help students understand the importance of "the disguise" in *The Merry Adventures of Robin Hood.*
2. To help students relate to the roguish tricks in the story.

MATERIALS: Materials from the classroom are not required for this activity.

PROCEDURE:

1. Throughout the story, Robin Hood refers to his "chest of strange garments," because Robin Hood and his merry men often disguised themselves in order to accomplish their goals. For example, Robin Hood disguised himself as a minstrel before the wedding. When Robin Hood attends the shooting match at Nottingham Town, he dressed as "a tattered stranger in scarlet, who wore a patch over one eye" while his merry men clothed themselves as tinkers, friars, peasants, beggars, etc.

2. In order to help students appreciate the purpose of these costumes, and the humorous situations they present, the teacher could declare a "Robin Hood and Merry Men Day." On that day, each student should be asked to come to school clothed in one of the "disguises" Robin Hood kept "in his chest of strange garments."

3. The teacher may wish to offer some suggestions to the students. Robin Hood's disguises included:
   a. Tattered stranger in scarlet at the shooting match.
   b. Will Stutely wears a friar's gown when he is rescued.
   c. The men dress as peasants, tinkers and beggars at the shooting match.
   d. Robin Hood turns butcher.
   e. Little John dresses all in scarlet to attend Nottingham Fair.
   f. Robin Hood dresses as a minstrel at the marriage.
   g. Little John dresses as a barefoot friar.
   h. Students could be encouraged to dress as Robin Hood himself.
   i. Robin Hood dressed as a beggar when he met the beggar.
   j. He dressed as a cobbler when he escaped from the King.
   k. Robin Hood dressed as Guy of Gisbourne.

4. While students are preparing their disguises, they should be encouraged to refer to the book itself for graphic descriptions. Also, students could refer to costume books for hints and suggestions. Accessories like feathers, ropes, bows, arrows, belts, etc., should be encouraged.

5. Once students are in costume, if weather permits, students could "feast" (eat their lunches) outdoors, Robin Hood style, among the trees.

BACKPACKING THROUGH SHERWOOD FOREST

OBJECTIVES:
1. To gain an understanding of the role the setting plays in the story.
2. To exercise visual awareness.

MATERIALS: Copy of picture on the illustration page and copy of the picture key of birds also on an illustration page.

PROCEDURE:
1. Discuss the fact that much of the action takes place in Sherwood Forest - a location thought to have been twenty miles long and eight miles wide. Although it was small by forest standards, it was large enough in which to hide from the Sheriff of Nottingham.

2. Point out to the class that the author chose a forest for the setting of this hide-and-seek because it had so many natural possibilities for camouflage. In fact, Pyle clothed Robin and his Merry Men all in Lincoln green so as to camouflage them. (Lincoln green was a bright green cloth named after the city in which it was made.)

3. Tell the class that they too will play a game of hide-and-seek in Sherwood Forest. It is the task of each class member to find the fourteen birds listed below hiding in the forest on the illustration page. Each student will have to do some research on the birds in order to be able to visually identify them.

   1. pheasant
   2. wood lark
   3. pullet
   4. daw
   5. bullfinch
   6. great blue heron
   7. wild pigeon
   8. merlin
   9. magpie
   10. starling
   11. capon
   12. falcon
   13. thrush
   14. throstle-cock

4. Distribute the picture key of birds to each student along with a copy of the double-paged picture of Sherwood Forest. See who can find all of the hidden birds and identify them.

5. The teacher may wish to extend the activity by playing a bird identification game. In this game one student is asked to verbally describe one of the fourteen birds while the rest of the class tries to identify it. The student who identifies the bird first gets to describe the next bird. This would be an excellent way to make use of the students' research.

BIRDS OF SHERWOOD FOREST

PULLET

STARLING

CAPON

HERON

DAW

THRUSH

BULLFINCH

MERLIN

WILD PIGEON

FALCON

THROSTLE-COCK

MAGPIE

WOOD LARK

PHEASANT

64

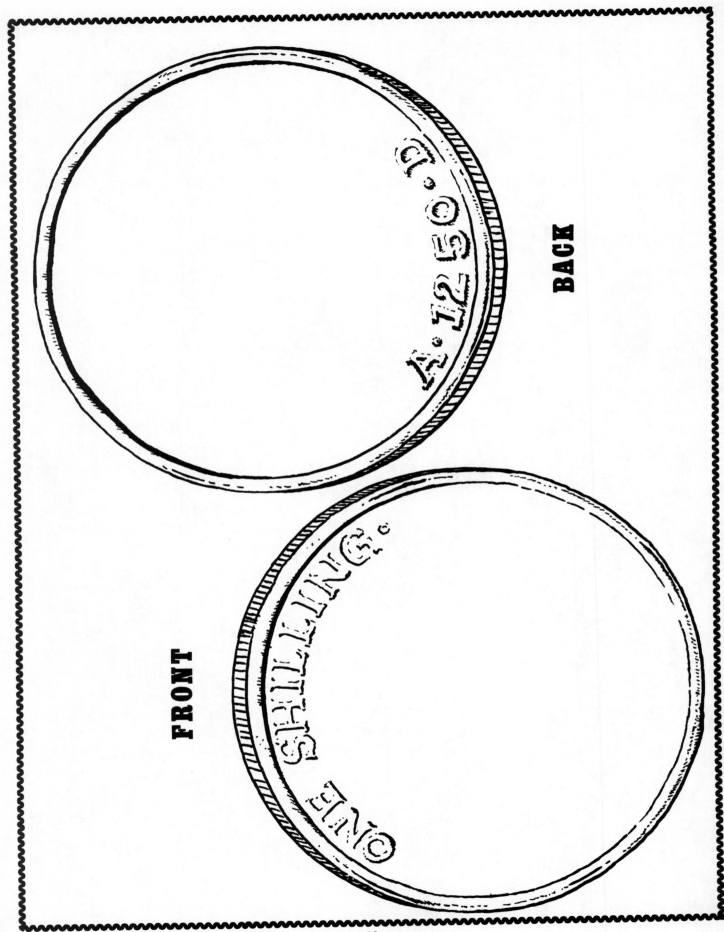

BACK

FRONT

ROBIN HOOD - A HERO FOR ALL SEASONS

OBJECTIVES:

1. To study the classic characteristics of heroism as they relate to the central figure.
2. To experience the opportunity to create visual art.

MATERIALS:

Paper, pencils, markers, and commemorative coin pattern on illustration page.

PROCEDURE:

1. Discuss in detail the classic characteristics of a "hero" - courage, loyalty, cleverness, vitality, and a defender of justice - and how they relate to Robin Hood.

   Robin Hood displays courage throughout the story. One example took place when he went to the shooting match at Nottingham Town even though he would be surrounded by enemies who had held the match for the express purpose of catching him.

   Robin Hood displayed loyalty when he refused to allow Will Stutely to be abandoned to the enemy. Furthermore, when Little John was wounded during Stutely's rescue, Robin refused to leave him.

   Robin Hood displayed cleverness when disguised as a butcher. He tricked the Sheriff of Nottingham out of $1,400.00 which then in turn was used to pay an unjust tax bill.

   Robin Hood displayed vitality throughout the story as his energy and optimism motivated the Merry Men. Furthermore, his expert handling of the longbow took great energy.

   Robin Hood displayed a constant fight for upholding the rights of the men against the unjust "forest laws." He robbed the rich and gave to the poor because the Norman rule was so oppressive. He was the champion of the Saxons!

2. Divide the class into five groups. Have each group design a commemorative coin in honor of one of Robin Hood's heroic characteristics.

3. As students are designing the coin, they should be reminded to stress one particular characteristic of a hero. Each coin should contain symbols and ideas from the story stressing that characteristic. Students could discuss that heroic trait as they present their coin to the class.

4. Coins could be displayed on a bulletin board.

PRINCIPLES OF THIEVES

OBJECTIVES:
1. To make students aware of the proverbs and morals throughout *The Merry Adventures of Robin Hood.*
2. To help students understand the meaning and function of proverbs and morals in the story.
3. To help students relate to the humor in the story.

MATERIALS:
Pencil, paper, copy of *Robin Hood*.

PROCEDURE:
1. Through example and definition, discuss proverbs and morals with the students. A moral, according to Webster, relates to "...principles of right and wrong," and a proverb is a "maxim...or general truth...rule of conduct." The very presence of morals and proverbs in *Robin Hood* is comical in itself. Imagine thieves and outlaws spouting rules and principles to one another. The context in which these morals and proverbs appear becomes quite humorous.
2. Point out to students that things like the Golden Rule: "Do unto others..." and "A penny saved..." and "Fools rush in..." are modern types of proverbs and morals.
3. Present some of these sayings from *The Merry Adventures of Robin Hood:*
   a. When Robin Hood speaks to David of Doncaster about the shooting match at Nottingham Town, he speaks about "hasty men and fools." (Point out to students that in essence Robin Hood is referring to the Sheriff as a fool, and eventually proves this.)
   b. Will Stutely is disguised as a poor friar when he stops at the Sign of the Blue Boar Inn. Eadom, the landlord, speaks about not kicking lame dogs in proverb. (Indicate to students that at least the landlord was fooled by the disguise.)
   c. The steward at the Sheriff's abode chides Little John about idle heads and empty stomachs. (Point out the great insult.)
   d. Robin Hood speaks to Will Scarlet when the two meet, about fat from overliving. (Another humorous insult.)
   e. Haste and butter churning are discussed by Will Scarlet when he discovers he is battling Robin Hood. (Will points out that haste makes waste.)
   f. Robin Hood refers to the many eyes of the world as he chides the Sorrowful Knight. (Here, Robin Hood points out that to some he is a thief, and to others he is an honorable man.)

g.   While lamenting the loss of his friends when he lost his fortune, the Sorrowful Knight speaks of oaks falling and swine running. (Point out that he infers that his friends are swine.)

h.   Saint Hubert is quoted in a proverb about saving breath to prevent a scalding mouth, as Sir Richard goes to pay his debts. (This is an interesting form of preventing foot-in-mouth.")

i.   Robin speaks about over-caution, when he appears before the queen. (A watched pot never....)

Discuss the meaning of each saying with your students, and see if class can place the saying in the context of the story: who said it? when? If not, give the students clues so they can understand the humor in these "morals."

4.   Once students grasp the "flavor" of statements of principle, perhaps the class could try writing some proverbs for the following circumstances:

a.   coming to school when ill: "He comes to school with a cold...etc."

b.   speaking without first raising your hand.

c.   neglecting to pay attention.

d.   disobeying your teacher.

e.   running in the halls.

5.   Students could share their proverbs with the class.

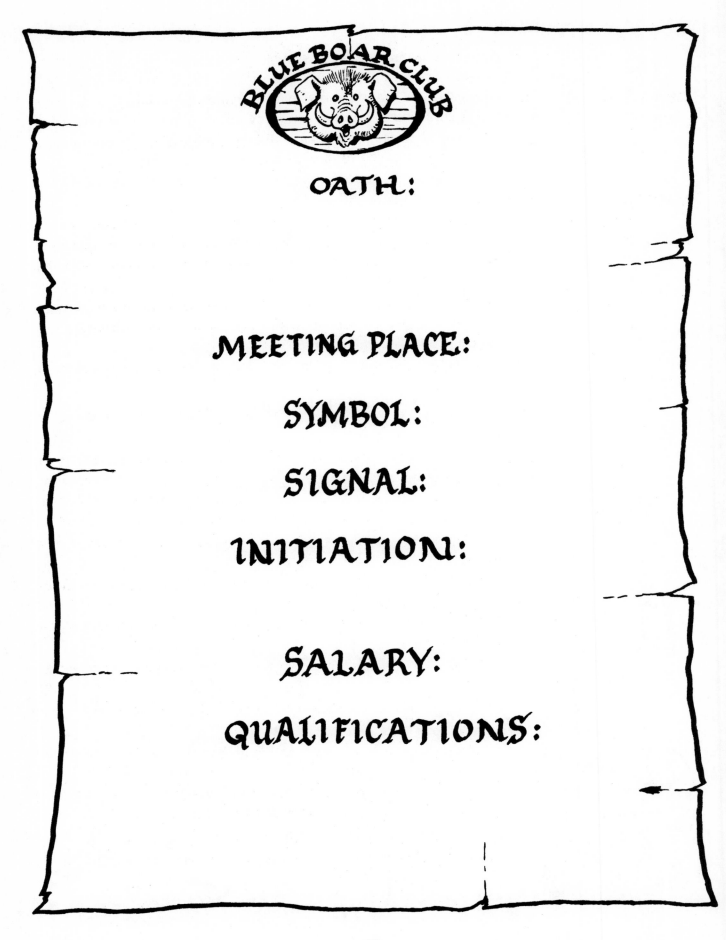

BLUE BOAR CLUB

OATH:

MEETING PLACE:

SYMBOL:

SIGNAL:

INITIATION:

SALARY:

QUALIFICATIONS:

CODE OF FRIENDSHIP

OBJECTIVES:

1. To help students relate to the strong comradery displayed by Robin Hood and his Merry band of men.
2. To help students understand the ramifications of loyalty and friendship displayed throughout the story.

MATERIALS: Various drawing materials, paper and pencil.

PROCEDURE:

1. Robin Hood and his men functioned as a group under the stipulations of both a formal oath and many unwritten understandings. Their loyalty and ability to communicate with humor and signals were uncanny. One sees evidence of their comradeship in every adventure. Discuss this friendship with your students, and ask students to find specific evidence from the book. Make sure students include the "magic" horn, the joyful competitions, and the ability to sense when others are in trouble.

2. To help students understand the ramifications of the relationship, divide them into groups of four. Each group will be asked to form a "Blue Boar Club." These students must set up codes, signals, signs, initiations, and forms of communication, to stimulate the "comradery" within Robin Hood's group, remembering that Robin Hood's men were essentially kind, good-natured people who wanted to be helpful.

3. Each group must develop the following ideas: (appropriate for the classroom)

   a. Oath: For ideas and reference see oath Robin Hood took when he came to be an outlaw.

   b. Meeting Place: Robin Hood used Sherwood Forest and the Blue Boar Inn.

   c. Symbol: Lincoln green suits were the symbol for Robin Hood's men.

   d. Signal: Three blasts on the horn called Robin Hood's men together.

   e. Initiation: For reference, refer to Little John's initiation when he came to be an outlaw.

   f. Salary: What would be appropriate "annual" payment for club members? (three suits of clothes and three meals a day)

   g. List of qualifications for club membership.

4. Each group could then present their club outline to the class.

ALLAN A DALE LIVES

OBJECTIVES: 1.   To study the literary form of the ballad.

                     2.   To experience creative writing.

MATERIALS: Pencil and paper.

PROCEDURE: 1.   Discuss the literary form of the ballad with the class. Tell the students that ballads were story songs like the one the Tanner sang to Robin entitled "The Wooing of Sir Keith." Emphasize to the students that the ballad tells a story simply, objectively and with lots of action. The melodies are often built around four short phrases arranged in an A B A B rhyme scheme. In other words, the first and third lines rhyme and the second and the fourth lines rhyme.

                     2.   Tell the students that they will assume the duties of Robin Hood's minstrel, Allan a Dale, and will write a ballad about one of the good outlaw's adventures. Ask the students to work in pairs and study the story to find an adventure to chronicle.

                     3.   When the students have selected an adventure, encourage them to write the ballad in stanzas of four phrases each. Also, remind them that the emphasis is the action, the problem and the solution. Furthermore, the balladeer can repeat a particularly dramatic line throughout the ballad if it is effective. Also, nonsense lines can be made up if they seem to fit, i.e., "with a high down down a downe."

                     4.   The pairs can share their ballads with the class by either reading them aloud in unison or singing them.

TRUE AND FALSE QUESTIONNAIRE
ROBIN HOOD

1. Some of the disguises Robin Hood used were butcher, beggar and minstrel.

2. The Sheriff of Nottingham was Robin Hood's best friend.

3. Robin Hood was a hero.

4. Robin Hood went to a shooting match at Nottingham Town even though he knew he would be surrounded by enemies who held the match for the express purpose of catching him.

5. *Robin Hood* is an autobiography.

6. Robin Hood was an expert at handling the longbow.

7. Robin Hood's men received a payment of three suits of clothes and three meals a day for each year they were part of his Merry Men.

8. Maid Marion was a main character in the book, and the action revolved around her.

9. Robin Hood and his men often met at the Red Robin Inn.

10. Three blasts on a horn called Robin Hood's men together.

11. Any old outlaw could become a member of Robin Hood's Merry Men.

12. Allan a Dale was a minstrel and wrote ballads.

13. Sherwood Forest was "home" for Robin Hood and his men.

14. Lincoln green was the color of the clothes Robin Hood and his men usually wore in the forest.

15. The Sheriff of Nottingham finally captured Robin Hood and sentenced him to life in prison.

16. Robin Hood robbed the rich and gave to the poor.

17. The Sheriff's steward and Little John finally became good friends.

18. The Sorrowful Knight lost his fortune but Robin Hood helped him get it back.

19. When moving through Sherwood Forest, Robin Hood always drove a covered wagon so he could keep his supplies with him at all times.

(1) T (2) F (3) T (4) T (5) F (6) T (7) T (8) F (9) F (10) T (11) F (12) T (13) T (14) T (15) F (16) T (17) F (18) T (19) F

HOWARD PYLE
1853 - 1911

BORN Howard Pyle was born on March 5, 1853, in Wilmington, Delaware.

FAMILY He was the son of William Pyle, the owner of a leather business. His mother, Margaret, was a painter.

CHILDHOOD He was introduced to quality books and art by his mother. She read aloud to him constantly from such literature as *Robinson Crusoe, Gulliver Among the Pygmies and Giants* and *Ivanhoe.* He drew pictures incessantly. In fact, when he attended school he fell short of the concentration needed to be a good student because he was preoccupied with filling his slate with pictures. The family decided to put him in art school to develop his talent.

CONTRIBUTIONS As an artist and illustrator, Howard Pyle gave children exceptionally beautiful pictures to enjoy. He illustrated not only his version of *Robin Hood* but also *King Arthur and His Knights. Howard Pyle's Book of Pirates* is very appealing.

INTERESTING FACT When Howard Pyle was eight years old he had the urge to write a poem. His mother gave him a pencil and a piece of gilded paper on which to do so. He found a quiet spot outside near a rock and tried to write. He could not do it. Pyle says that that was the most frustrating feeling he had ever felt.

EPITAPH OR FINAL THOUGHT Pyle died on November 9, 1911, in Florence, Italy. He felt that the key to success depended on having ceaseless industry, ambition of purpose, enthusiasm and imagination.

TREASURE ISLAND

ROBERT LOUIS STEVENSON

A TREASURE HUNTING WE WILL GO

OBJECTIVES:
1. To reinforce map making and reading skills.
2. To help students relate to the "mystery" in *Treasure Island.*
3. To help students relate to the excitement of finding a "treasure."

MATERIALS: Shiny tokens or something of value to students that could be buried, rulers, pencils, markers, compass, school grounds, poster board.

PROCEDURE:
1. Briefly review basic map skills with students including signs, symbols, directions, key, and scale. Discuss the concept of "clues." Review compass directions, and help students relate north, south, east, and west to your school setting.

2. Divide class into groups of three. Give each group some tokens, and allow the groups private time to bury their tokens on the school grounds. Each group should bury tokens.

3. Once the tokens are hidden, ask each group to draw a map of the playground. Students should be encouraged to create their own key, symbols, and if possible, even scale. Each group should be working in a private area.

4. When maps are completed, the groups should create "clue" sheets to accompany their maps. Remind students that clues should be subtle and should relate to their maps, symbols, and key. The clues should help other people find the "hidden treasure."

5. Once the clue sheets are completed, groups should trade maps and clues in order to discover one another's treasures.

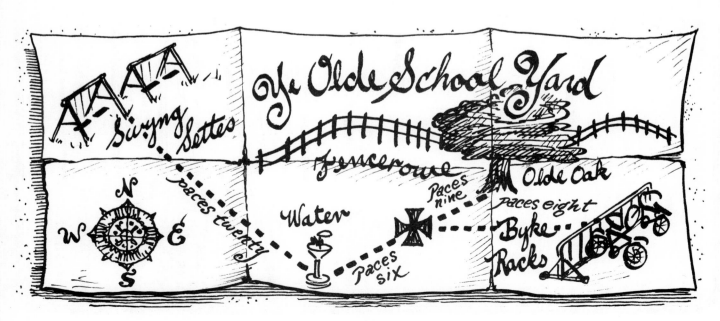

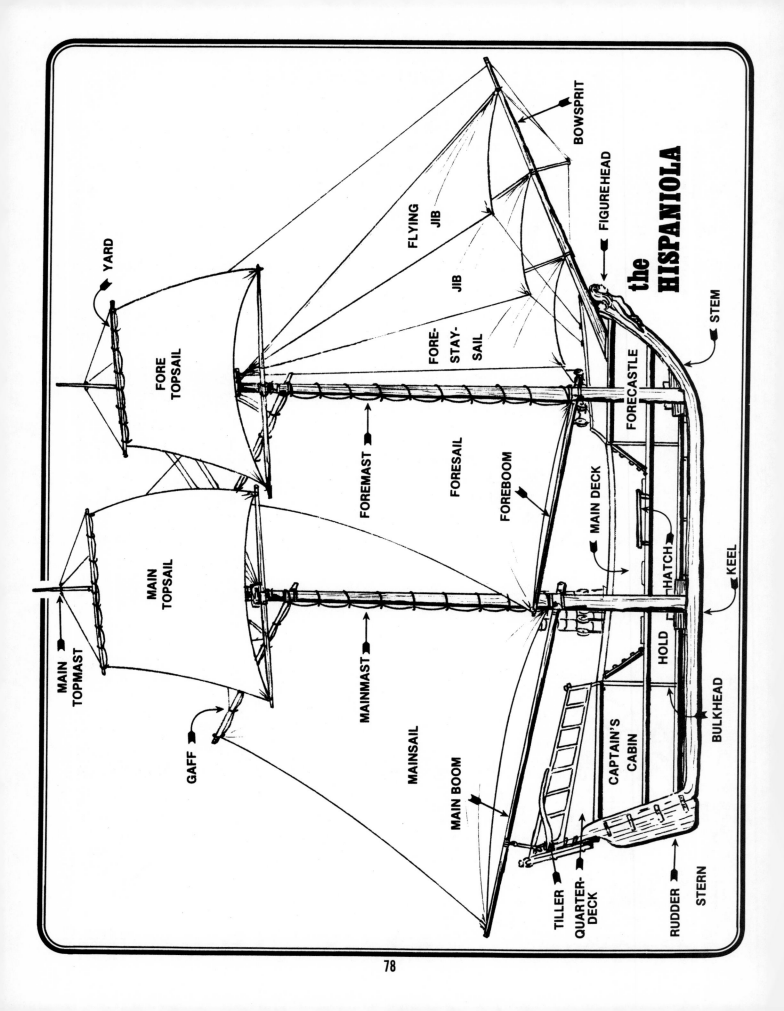

the **HISPANIOLA**

BOWSPRIT

FIGUREHEAD

STEM

FLYING JIB

JIB

FORE-STAY-SAIL

FORECASTLE

YARD

FORE TOPSAIL

FOREMAST

FORESAIL

FOREBOOM

MAIN DECK

HATCH

KEEL

MAIN TOPSAIL

MAINMAST

MAINSAIL

MAIN BOOM

HOLD

CAPTAIN'S CABIN

BULKHEAD

MAIN TOPMAST

GAFF

TILLER

QUARTER-DECK

RUDDER

STERN

WORD AHOY

OBJECTIVES:

1. To help students develop an understanding of the nautical and geographical terms used throughout *Treasure Island.*
2. To help students review parts of speech, alphabetizing, and use of the dictionary.
3. To give students an opportunity to increase vocabulary by using context clues.

MATERIALS:

Paper, pencil, drawing paper, crayons, markers and cardboard and materials for making books, optional.

PROCEDURES:

1. Throughout *Treasure Island*, Stevenson uses many nautical and geographical terms, all of which contribute to the mood of the story. These terms include words like:

schooners	keel-hauling	ebb
berth	inlets	island
cove	topsails	peaks steersman
hoist	spyglass	cruise
hulk	plank	mutiny
fathom	decks	main-hold
mariner	seafaring	figureheads
pirate	mate	seaworthy
boatswain	docks	rudder
nautical	latitude	shipmate
skipper	longitude	swabs
stern	craft	riggers
tide	crew	jibs maroon
coxswain	bays	cabin boy

2. At any point in the story, the teacher could introduce some or all of these terms to students either through discussion or list.
3. Students should be asked to separate nautical from geographical terms.
4. Each student should then be asked to make either a nautical or geographical dictionary with illustrations. Each student must alphabetize, define and illustrate each word.
5. Dictionaries could be used for reference while story is completed.

THE PARROTING OF LONG JOHN SILVER

OBJECTIVES: 1.   To develop listening skills in relation to vocal volume, rate and interpretation.

                    2.   To discover how mood is communicated vocally.

MATERIALS: The list of Long John Silver quotations shown below.

PROCEDURE: 1.   Divide the class into pairs. Ask one partner to take the role of Long John Silver and the other to take the role of his parrot, Captain Flint.

                    2.   Long John Silver will interpret each line below according to the attached mood. The parrot will echo the words in an effort to match volume, rate and interpretation. Be sure to encourage every student to feel the emotion attached to the line. Feel mad when Silver is mad; feel boastful when Silver is boastful and feel angry when Silver is angry.

1. Shiver me timbers, so here's that very Jim Hawkins! (SURPRISE)
2. Aye, aye, mates, come and have a little yarn with John. (FRIENDLY)
3. I calls my parrot Cap'n in honor of the famous buccaneer. (PROUD)
4. Them that die'll be the lucky ones. (ANGRY)
5. Take a cutlass, and I'll see the color of his blood. (MEAN)
6. Belay me hearties, don't you dare cross a ghostly spirit. (WARNING)
7. You're a good lad. You saved my life and I'll not forget it. (SINCERE)
8. Batten down your hatches till you're spoke to, you old sea dog. (MAD)

80

SPENDING THE BOOTY

OBJECTIVES:

1. To exercise the imagination by extending the story.
2. To have an opportunity to reflect, fantasize and prioritize how to spend a fortune.

MATERIALS: Pencils and a ledger sheet.

PROCEDURE:

1. Remind the class that there were five survivors of this adventure - Jim Hawkins, Captain Smollett, Gray, Dr. Livesey and Ben Gunn. The story tells the reader that Captain Smollett was able to retire on his share of the treasure. Gray saved part of his money and used part of it for study. He then purchased a fine fully rigged ship. Ben Gunn, on the other hand, spent or lost his in three weeks and became a beggar.

2. Ask the students what they think Jim Hawkins did with his share of the treasure after he returned home. In other words, how did the treasure affect the rest of his life?

3. Next, ask the students what they each would do with one million dollars if they were to suddenly come into possession of this sum.

4. Pass out a ledger sheet to each student to fill out a budget for one million dollars. Encourage the students to think of both short-term (records, bikes, etc.) and long-term (college, a car) economic goals. Have them research the cost of items whenever they are not sure. Also, have them think about the problem of inflation. For instance, what will a college education cost by the time students are ready for it?

5. Those students who choose to save a portion of the million dollars should be encouraged to compute the interest on the money that will be incurred, using current interest rates.

ON THE DECK OF THE HISPANIOLA

OBJECTIVES:

1. To capture the pirates' feelings for oral tradition via song.
2. To experience the rhythm inherent in the combination of mime, movement, and song.

MATERIALS:

Collected bandanas, gold earrings, eye patches, makeup pencils for drawing scars, mustaches, tatoos and a cleared area in which to work.

PROCEDURE:

1. Tell the students that sailors have always been people who practiced oral tradition - the handing down of tales and yarns via storytelling and song from one generation to another.
2. Have the entire class practice one such oral tradition found in *Treasure Island* entitled "Fifteen men on the dead man's chest." Encourage the class to chant/sing the lyrics with lots of energy and robust sounds in unison.
3. With collected bandanas, eye patches and gold earrings, ask each student to transform into a pirate. Encourage the adding of scars, mustaches, tatoos and the blackening of teeth.
4. Divide the class of pirates into work details for mime - one group could swab the decks, another group could man the oars, the third group could hoist the Jolly Roger and the fourth group could coil ropes. A volunteer could hobble around on deck as Long John Silver.
5. After practicing the movement involved in each mime, ask all groups to take positions on the floor and begin the mimes while chanting the song in unison.

TREASURE ISLAND ALBUM

OBJECTIVES:
1. To make students aware of Stevenson's masterful use of description.
2. To help students "picture" the characters and scenes in the story.

MATERIALS: Cardboard, paper, crayons, or magic markers.

PROCEDURE:
1. Stevenson was a master of description. *Treasure Island* is filled with tales of villainous pirates and innocent gentlefolk. Many of the characters and events are described so vividly that detailed portraits can be painted.
2. Tell students that they are going to make a Treasure Island album. This album will be filled with pictures created by students using Stevenson's descriptions which appear throughout *Treasure Island.* Interesting portraits might include: "The old brown seaman," Black Dog, Blind Man, Long John Silver and Ben Gunn. Interesting scenes might include Black Dog and Old Seaman Duel, The Black Spot, The Sea-Chest, *Hispaniola,* Apple Barrel, The Island, The Log-House, Israel Hands' Battle, The Treasure Hunt.
3. Students could be divided into groups of two or three, and after the class has decided upon a format, each group could draw a "photo" to be placed in the album. Remind students that the pictures should rely on Stevenson's descriptions.
4. Album could be left on display throughout the teaching unit.

TRUE AND FALSE QUESTIONNAIRE
TREASURE ISLAND

1. *Pieces of Eight* was the name of the ship Jim Hawkins and Long John Silver took to Treasure Island.

2. Captain Flint was the name of Long John Silver's parrot.

3. At the end of the story, Ben Gunn became a beggar.

4. Black Spot was the name of Jim Hawkins' dog.

5. Robert Louis Stevenson is the author of *Treasure Island*.

6. At the beginning of the story, Jim Hawkins and his parents managed the Admiral Benbow Inn.

7. Black Dog killed the captain who was staying at the Admiral Benbow Inn.

8. Jim Hawkins found the treasure map hidden in the bushes behind the Inn.

9. The treasure map revealed an island that was nine miles long and five miles wide. The island had two harbors.

10. Dr. Livesey offered to outfit a ship by himself and help search for the treasure.

11. Jim Hawkins served as a cabin boy on the *Hispaniola*.

12. Long John Silver was hired to serve as the Captain on the *Hispaniola*.

13. At the end of the story, Jim Hawkins purchased a fully rigged ship with his portion of the treasure.

14. Long John Silver was a very strong man whose left leg had been cut off at the hip.

15. The song "Fifteen Men on the Dead Man's Chest" was sung by the crew on the *Hispaniola*.

16. Captain Smollett and Squire Trelawney did not trust each other.

17. Jim was hiding in a pickle barrel when he heard of Long John Silver's planned mutiny.

18. Spy-glass was the name of the tallest hill on Treasure Island.

19. Jim Hawkins first met Ben Gunn in Bristol before the *Hispaniola* headed toward Treasure Island.

(1) F (2) T (3) T (4) F (5) T (6) T (7) F (8) F (9) T (10) F (11) T (12) F (13) F (14) T (15) T (16) T (17) F (18) T (19) F

ROBERT LOUIS STEVENSON
1850 - 1894

BORN Robert Louis Stevenson was born in Scotland on November 13, 1850.

FAMILY Stevenson's father, Thomas Stevenson, was a prominent engineer. His mother was Margaret Balfour.

CHILDHOOD Stevenson, nicknamed "Little Lou," was a sickly child who spent many months in bed every time the cold Edinburgh wind blew. Consequently, he did not enjoy the company of other children. In fact, his fragile health kept him from playing sports. His peer group made fun of him for wanting to sit around dreaming and writing.

CONTRIBUTIONS Stevenson, a poet and novelist, is most beloved by generations of children for his adventure stories and poetry. *A Child's Garden of Verses* originally entitled *Penny Whistles* and *Treasure Island* have been translated into many languages.

INTERESTING FACT Stevenson, one day, drew a map of an island to entertain his stepson. The map then needed a story. The story written to accompany the map was *Treasure Island.*

EPITAPH OR FINAL THOUGHTS

Under the wide and starry sky,
Dig the grave and let me die,
Glad did I live and gladly die,
And I laid me down with a will.

ROBINSON CRUSOE

DANIEL DEFOE

JOURNAL

Name _____ Date _____

Location _____

Reflections _____

_____

_____

_____

_____

_____

_____

_____

_____

_____

_____

_____

WRITTEN REFLECTIONS

OBJECTIVES: 1. To give students experiences in journal writing.

2. To help students understand the purposes and techniques of journal composition.

MATERIALS: Paper, pencil, spiral notebooks (optional).

PROCEDURE:

1. When Robinson Crusoe arrived on the island, he kept a journal to help him keep track of time. This journal served as a record of his thoughts, feelings and daily activities. It was this journal, apparently, that helped him recount his adventure.

2. Discuss the ramifications of journal writing with the students. Be certain to remind students that journals are not simply listings of events, but rather ideas, thoughts, reactions, and emotions. For example, a journal entry would not simply state, "I met a new friend today. He is nice." It might say, "I met a kid named Johnny Smith today. He seemed friendly, but I don't think Mom will like him because his table manners aren't so hot. I hope the other kids like him...maybe he could come to the party tomorrow. I think I'll ask him. I wonder if he could help me with my math."

3. Other points to be discussed about journal writing should include:
    a. Journals are personal and can include your most private thoughts.
    b. Because journals are personalized, punctuation, spelling, etc., need not be emphasized. Journals are not written for an audience, but for the writer.
    c. Journal entries should be dated and done in ink.
    d. Journal entries should be made 4-5 times per week.
    e. Journals should be like written-down speech.

4. Ask your students to keep journals for 2-3 weeks. In order to maintain the spirit of a journal, these books should not be collected or corrected unless the student requests it. Instead, just have students show evidence of completion by flipping through the pages.

5. Students should be encouraged to continue with their journals throughout the year.

CRUSOE'S CONDO ISLAND

OBJECTIVES:
1. To heighten awareness of the setting of the story.
2. To exercise the imagination.

MATERIALS: Pencils, paper, markers, poster board, paste, colored paper.

PROCEDURE:
1. Discuss the fact that Robinson Crusoe felt like he was lord and master over the entire island. He owned all of its resources and land. If he had been amidst civilization he would have been a wealthy man.

2. Ask the class to imagine that Crusoe, upon returning to England, decides to develop the island by building and selling condominiums on it. The students' task is to prepare a brochure displaying the island's most attractive selling points.

3. Have the students go through the story and make a list of the island's features such as size, shape, topography, climate, animal habitation, types of flowers, trees and so on.

4. Students may work in pairs or small groups to put together an attractive real estate brochure using a variety of art supplies.

KEEPING TRACK OF TIME

OBJECTIVES: 1.   To exercise the imagination.

2.   To experience creative problem solving.

MATERIALS: Pencils and paper.

PROCEDURE: 1.   Remind the students that Robinson Crusoe was on his island for twenty-eight years, two months and nineteen days! Defoe tells the reader that Crusoe kept track of the days by making a mark each day on a large wooden cross.

2.   Ask the class to first calculate how many marks would have been made by the end of his island stay using the above figures.

3.   Next, suggest to students that this method of keeping track of time was very impractical. Note the number of days that marks would have been put on the wooden cross. Arrange the class into groups of nine. Each group must come up with a better way for Crusoe to keep track of time than the method devised by Defoe.

4.   During brainstorming, encourage the students to "play" with ideas in an accepting environment. In other words, all members of each group should feel free to say whatever comes to mind with absolutely no fear of rejection. All ideas are good. The more ideas generated the better the chances are that the group will come up with a useful way to keep track of time on Crusoe's island.

NECESSITY IS THE MOTHER OF INVENTION

OBJECTIVES:

1. To gain an understanding of how Crusoe's necessity was the mother of his invention.

2. To develop a sense of invention via transforming objects and materials.

MATERIALS:

Found objects and discarded materials brought from home, discovered on the playground and found in junk piles.

PROCEDURE:

1. Discuss the situation that Robinson Crusoe found himself in when he first landed on the island with no shelter, food, clothing or tools.

2. Point out how his need for these things caused him to transform every scrap of material into something useful by adding to it, subtracting from it or in some way transforming its size, shape or use. For instance, Crusoe fashioned an umbrella out of goatskin, a seine out of cloth and a basket out of twigs.

3. Ask the students to bring five discarded items or found objects from home (coat hangers, strips of cloth, rags, ribbons, pieces of wood, old kites, jars, old toys, straws).

4. These items should be placed in the middle of the room to form a "junk pile."

5. Have the students go to the junk pile and select items with which to make something useful. Encourage them to think of one of Crusoe's needs and go about to invent something to meet the need. (Make sure it is an item not invented in the book.)

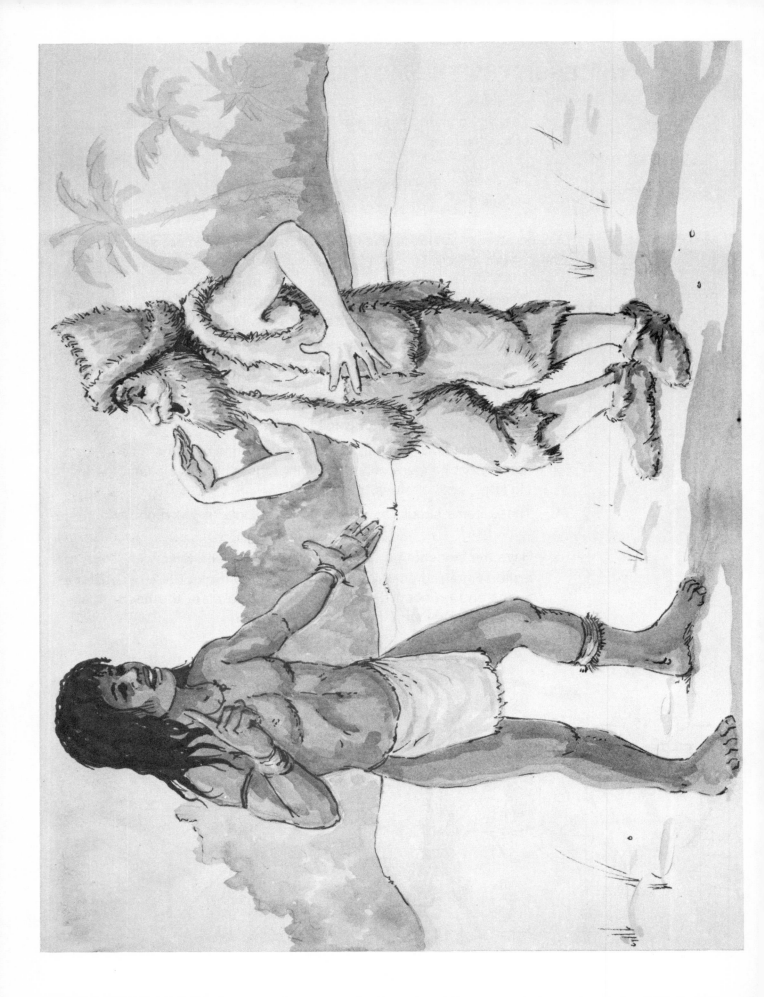

"PRINTS" OF AN INTRUDER

OBJECTIVES:

1. To stress the importance of the "footprint," and how it influenced Crusoe's life on the island.

2. To help students identify the frustration Crusoe felt when trying to identify the print.

3. To help children relate to the mystery and adventure in the book.

MATERIALS: Washable black paint, mural paper or poster board.

PROCEDURE:

1. When Robinson Crusoe discovered the footprint in the sand, he went into hiding for two years. His fears of an intruder seemed to dominate his existence. Before the realization that the print was indeed one of a human being, Crusoe studied it carefully and was able to determine **only** that it was not his own print.

2. In order for students to understand the difficulty in gleaning information from just a footprint, the teacher could ask each student to draw his own footprint on a large sheet of mural paper to form tracks. Encourage the students to wear a variety of shoe types such as tennis shoes, sandals, clogs, hiking boots, loafers and cowboy boots.

3. This mural of tracks could be used for an "identification" game. Have students attempt to match the footprints with the class member and shoe type. Students should discover, as did Crusoe, that footprints offer few clues to the naked eye about identity.

SILENT TALK

OBJECTIVES:

1. To help students understand the difficulties Crusoe had establishing a relationship with Friday, a man with no language.

2. To give students experiences in charades.

MATERIALS: None.

PROCEDURE:

1. When Crusoe saved Friday, a friendship developed between the two men. However, as Defoe indicates, the initial stages of that friendship were difficult because Friday was like a savage and could not speak Crusoe's language. Friday had to communicate his thanks, and Crusoe had to communicate his friendship without using words.

2. Ask students to role play the two men and communicate without language. At first, during the role-playing activity, the teacher may wish to have students communicate specific ideas to each other. For example, Friday might charade things like: "Thank you! Who are you? Where do you live? It was kind of you to save me." Crusoe might be asked to charade things like: "How did you get here? Who are you? Are you a friend or foe? How do I know I can trust you? etc."

3. Once the students understand the possibilities in nonverbal communication, perhaps two students could be asked to charade a conversation between Crusoe and Friday, while other students guess the nature of the conversation.

TRUE AND FALSE QUESTIONNAIRE
ROBINSON CRUSOE

1. Robinson Crusoe's parents were pleased when he went to the sea because they wanted him to be a famous explorer.

2. When Crusoe was going to Africa to bring slaves back to his plantation, he was the only survivor of a shipwreck.

3. Robinson Crusoe kept a journal of his activities beginning with the day he arrived on his island.

4. Crusoe was on his island for 28 years, 2 months and 19 days.

5. The young man kept track of time with a small calendar he retrieved from the shipwreck.

6. After living on the island for about 15 years, Crusoe discovered a man's footprint in the sand.

7. At the end of the story, Crusoe returned to England, but had to leave Friday on the island.

8. Friday was a small goat that Crusoe tamed and kept as a pet.

9. Daniel Defoe was the author of *Robinson Crusoe.*

10. Crusoe had to provide for all of his own basic needs: food, shelter, clothing.

11. Friday was a savage who spoke English amazingly well when Crusoe first met him.

12. A group of cannibals visited Crusoe's island.

13. When Crusoe returned home, he never went out to sea again.

14. Crusoe built one home on the island and stayed there year around because exploring was dangerous.

15. When Crusoe returned to England after his stay on the island, he learned he had become a wealthy man.

16. When Crusoe first landed on the island, he had a knife, a pipe and a waterproofed bag full of food with him.

17. Crusoe made a tent out of part of a sail he saved from the wrecked ship.

18. Money was very useful to Crusoe while he was on the island.

19. Robinson Crusoe ate goat meat while on the island.

(1) F (2) T (3) T (4) T (5) F (6) T (7) F (8) F (9) T (10) T (11) F (12) T (13) F (14) F (15) T (16) F (17) T (18) F (19) T

DANIEL DEFOE
1660-1731

BORN Daniel Defoe was born around 1660 in England.

FAMILY Defoe's father, James Foe, was a poor butcher and candlemaker. Since the family did not belong to the Church of England, Defoe was not allowed to attend Oxford University. Consequently, he was forced to go to a Dissenting Academy.

CHILDHOOD As a child Defoe saw London go up in flames. This made a lasting impression on him. Although he studied for the Presbyterian ministry, he elected not to follow this career. He owned a clothing store in London prior to becoming involved in politics and writing.

CONTRIBUTIONS Robinson Crusoe was published in 1719. It was immediately popular. This popularity is still evident today. This book was made into a film called *The Adventures of Robinson Crusoe* in 1953. A Disney film was produced in 1966 entitled *Lt. Robin Crusoe, USN.*

INTERESTING FACT As a novelist, journalist and pamphleteer Defoe often ran counter to the political power of the day. In fact, he was imprisoned for his thoughts contained in a pamphlet entitled *The Shortest Way with Dissenters*. He was placed in Newgate Prison a number of times for his writings.

EPITAPH OR FINAL THOUGHT Defoe died at the age of seventy on April 26, 1731, in Moorfields, London, England. He was buried in Bunhill Fields. At the time of his death he was heavily in debt as he was most of his lifetime.

KING ARTHUR

AND HIS

KNIGHTS OF THE

ROUND TABLE

SIR THOMAS MALORY

FEAST FIT FOR A KNIGHT

OBJECTIVES:

1. To understand the significance of and bountiful nature of the "feast" during the Age of Chivalry.

2. To understand the components of, and traditions inherent in, a feast.

MATERIALS:

Food like grapes, grape juice, apples, pears, English walnuts, chicken legs, fish, and cakes for dessert. Use plastic knives only for utensils. Serve on a long table with white tablecloth, serving platters and plates and wine goblets for all students.

PROCEDURE:

1. King Arthur and his knights partook in many feasts. There were feasts on Whitsunday, the High Feast of the Pentecost, and often feasts celebrating achievements of the knights. Each feast had much pomp and circumstance surrounding it, and there was a great deal of tradition involved in each meal.

2. Your students could plan and participate in one of these grand banquets. In planning for the banquet, each student could volunteer to contribute some of the food (listed in materials), and the teacher could include any or all of the following traditions common to feasts in Arthur's time:

   a. Great quantities of food were served and consumed.
   b. The only utensils knights used while eating were knives they kept in their belts.
   c. Antics by the court jester or clown were performed throughout the meal to entertain the knights. One or two students may wish to be court jesters.
   d. Each course of the meal was presented with much fanfare. A parade of servants carried the platters out as they were announced by trumpets.
   e. A "steward" supervised all activities making sure there were no lazy servants.
   f. Each pair of knights shared a wooden platter.
   g. The knights' platters were filled by their squires.
   h. During the feast, a singing minstrel would enter with an important message.
   i. Once a year, knights traded places with their squires, and their squires were served dinner. This day was called the Feast of Saint Stephen.

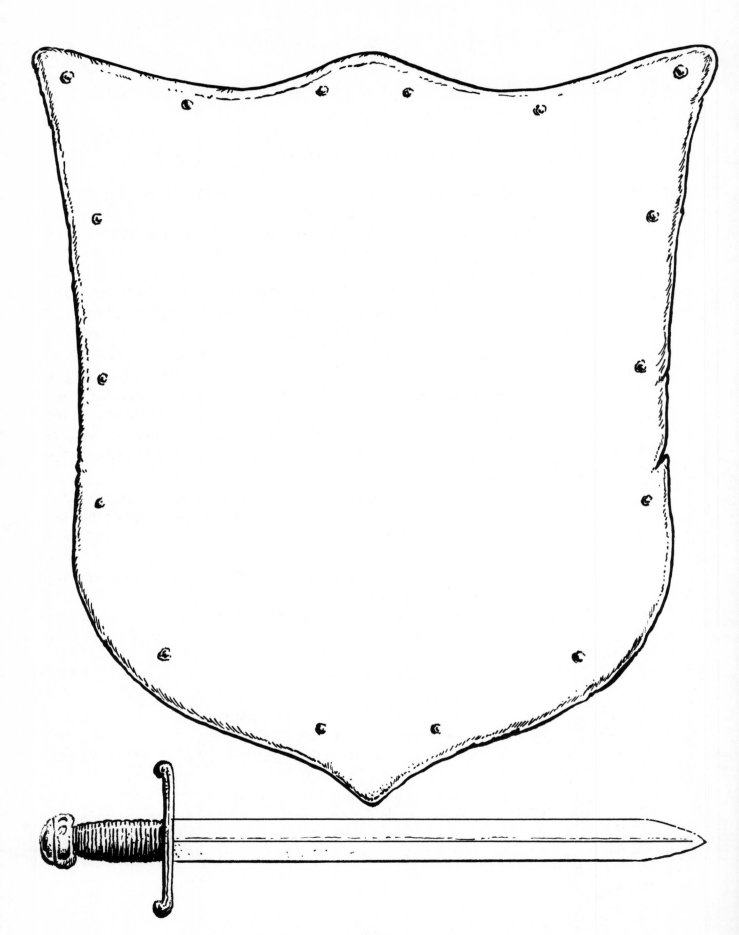

ONLY THE SHIELD KNOWS

OBJECTIVES:

1. To help students relate to the character traits of individual knights in *King Arthur*.
2. To help students understand the significance of battle in *King Arthur*.
3. To encourage creative thinking.

MATERIALS:

Shield outline on illustration page, pencils, crayons, magic markers.

PROCEDURE:

1. Discuss the many instances of mistaken or confused identity in *King Arthur*. Many of these instances occur during battle. For example, Pellinore did not know he was jousting with King Arthur by the fountain; everyone thought Sir Gareth, Beaumains, was a boy of the kitchen; nobody knew that it was Tristram who smote down Palamides; Tristram did not know he fought Lancelot.

2. Tell students that it is their charge to design shields that would identify people in the story, and thus prevent mistakes. That is, students must custom design a shield for any character in *King Arthur*. This shield design should reflect some personality trait that is evident in the character who will wear it. For example, a custom-made shield for Lancelot might reveal what a fine jouster he is. A shield for King Arthur might reveal him as head of the Round Table, etc.

3. When students complete shields for the characters in the story, the teacher might ask each student to design one for himself or a friend. Encourage students to create designs that represent personality traits.

4. These shields could be displayed in the classroom, and students might enjoy guessing the "owners."

THE ORDER OF THE ROUND TABLE

OBJECTIVES:

1. To emphasize the main idea behind King Arthur's Round Table.

2. To promote the "doing" of good deeds by class members.

MATERIALS:

Enough hardback chairs so that all class members can sit in a circle, same number of strips of cardboard 11" x 2" in size, six or seven tables (optional), colored tissue paper to make garlands and scarves to make headbands as shown on illustration page.

PROCEDURE:

1. Explain to the class that King Arthur received the Round Table from Guinevere's father as a wedding present. This made him extremely happy because he wished to have all his knights seated in equality with no head or foot to the arrangement. The table could seat one hundred and fifty knights. Here they would meet to openly share their latest good deeds with one another.

2. Ask the class to discuss the good deeds performed by the knights in the story. Ask the students to imagine what good deeds would be performed if the knights lived in today's world.

3. Instruct each of the students to undertake a "good deed" over the weekend and be prepared to tell all about it on Monday as they sit at the Round Table.

4. Prior to Monday's session, position the chairs in a complete circle. Tape each student's name to the back of the chair seats as were the names of the knights at King Arthur's Round Table. Be sure to place "Sir" in front of the boys' names and "Lady" in front of the girls' names. (If tables are available, place six or seven as needed in a circle so that the students can sit at a somewhat Round Table, optional.)

5. Have the boys make medieval headbands and the girls medieval garlands for their hair as shown in the illustration.

6. Ask each student to put on a headband or garland before taking the proper seat.

7. Go all around the circle as each knight and each lady tells of the good deed he/she has performed.

KING ARTHUR'S WAX MUSEUM

OBJECTIVES: 1.   To gain an understanding of the role played by the major characters in the story.

2.   To dramatize each character's role.

MATERIALS: A letter, a walking stick, a shield, Excalibur, Holy Grail, crown, harp, jar of colored water.

PROCEDURE: 1.   Tell the class that they are going to create a wax museum with the characters from the story. Ask the class to get into groups of three. One student will be the statue, the second student will be the sculptor who puts the statue in an identifying position and the third student will write up an information card to be placed next to the statue that explains who it is and what he did in the story.

2.   Eight statues that deserve to be placed in the museum and the identifying prop or posture to be used could be as follows:
   King Arthur (pulling Excalibur out of the stone)
   Queen (tied at the stake)
   Sir Lancelot (standing proudly with shield)
   Sir Galahad (reaching for the Holy Grail)
   Tristram (playing a harp)
   Morgana or Morgan le Fay (chanting over a potion of colored water)
   The Fair Maid Elaine of Astolat (lying dead with a letter in her hand)
   Merlin (standing with a magical walking stick)

3.   Once the statues have been positioned and the information cards have been placed, other classes can be taken on a tour through the museum.

CAMELOT COLLAGE

OBJECTIVES:

1. To emphasize the ideals upon which Arthur based his rule.

2. To experience transforming these ideals into visual concepts.

MATERIALS:

A variety of magazines, scissors, paste, heavyweight drawing paper and markers.

PROCEDURE:

1. Play the song "Camelot" from the Broadway show album entitled *Camelot.* Tell the class that this was Lerner and Lowe's idea of what Arthur's Camelot was like. Ask students to discuss what Arthur's idea of Camelot was as shown in the story. Focus in on such things as justice, honor, courage, plenty, peace, etc.

2. Next, ask each student to think about the possible characteristics of a modern day Camelot. These characteristics should be personal and reflect the point of view of each student.

3. Have the students find visual images of these concepts in the magazines provided. Cut and paste the images in order to form a Camelot collage as depicted in the illustration.

PROMISE OF KNIGHTHOOD

OBJECTIVES:
1. To help students relate to all aspects of chivalry and knighthood in King Arthur's time.

2. To give students experiences in creative writing and creative thinking.

3. To help students understand the meaning of a code of ethics.

MATERIALS: Paper and pencil.

PROCEDURE:
1. In order to become Knights of the Round Table, men had to take an oath and vows were renewed yearly. In that oath, men promised to undertake the obligations necessary to become fine and honorable knights. A specific oath is never stated in the book, but the reader is given many indications of the duties of a true knight throughout the story. These duties include things like helping a damsel in distress, doing boons when asked, never refusing to do battle, always being honorable and honest, defending what is good and honorable, etc.

2. Students should be divided into groups of three or four. Each group could represent a committee working for King Arthur. This committee should be "charged" with writing the "Oath of Knighthood" that was administered to each aspiring knight. Students may wish to write this code on a scroll and read it to the class.

3. This activity might also be modernized. That is, students could be asked to write an oath admitting them to the "Order of Gentlemen" or the "Order of Gentlewomen" in modern times. These oaths could be shared with the class.

TRUE AND FALSE QUESTIONNAIRE
KING ARTHUR

1. Arthur proved he was the rightful King of England by pulling a sword out of a stone.
2. Merlin was a magician.
3. "Excalibur" was the name of King Arthur's fearless horse.
4. Guinevere's father gave King Arthur the round table that had places for 150 knights as a wedding present.
5. King Arthur was able to fill the round table immediately because noble knights were easy to find.
6. Beaumains defeated the Black Knight, the Green Knight and the Red Knight.
7. Noble Knights of the Round Table would not defend women because the knights were too busy helping King Arthur.
8. Sir Lancelot refused to make Sir Galahad a Knight of the Round Table.
9. Sir Thomas Malory is the author of *King Arthur and the Knights of the Round Table.*
10. The Holy Grail was the drinking vessel used by Jesus Christ at the Last Supper.
11. None of the Noble Knights wished to search for the Holy Grail.
12. Sir Lancelot found the Holy Grail, but never returned to Camelot.
13. At the end of the story when Excalibur was thrown into the water, the sword rusted immediately.
14. The Excalibur had an "enchanted" scabbard that protected King Arthur.
15. Merlin helped King Arthur make many decisions.
16. Sir Galahad never returned after his quest for the Holy Grail.
17. Mordred's army defeated King Arthur.
18. Sir Lancelot refused to help King Arthur fight Mordred's army.
19. Many victories and celebrations were honored with great feasts.

(1) T (2) T (3) F (4) T (5) F (6) T (7) F (8) F (9) T (10) T (11) F (12) F (13) F (14) T (15) T (16) T (17) T (18) F (19) T

SIR THOMAS MALORY
c. 1400 - 1471

BORN Sir Thomas Malory was born in Newbold Revell, Warwickshire, England.

FAMILY Malory's father, Sir John Malory, lived in Warwickshire and died in 1434. His entire estate went to his son. Malory married and had a son of his own who died at an early age.

LIFE Malory fought in the War of the Roses and was a member of Parliament in 1445. Unfortunately, between 1450-1470 he was in and out of prison on a variety of charges.

CONTRIBUTION While in prison, Malory wrote the prose that has been used as the source for so many versions and adaptations entitled *Morte d'Arthur.* It was based on oral legends which went back as far as the 6th century. Malory's writing was divided into eight prose tales influenced by the French romances.

INTERESTING FACT *Morte d'Arthur* was one of the first books ever printed in English. William Caxton took the manuscript of eight tales after Malory died and published them as a single volume.

EPITAPH OR FINAL THOUGHTS Sir Thomas Malory died of the plague in 1471. His epitaph read: "praye for me whyle I am on lyne that God sende me good delyverance."

GULLIVER'S TRAVELS

JONATHAN SWIFT

THE GIANT GULLIVER FLOOR PATTERN

OBJECTIVES:

1. To experience the Lilliputians' amazement and wonder at the enormity of Gulliver's size.

2. To engage in math experiences of measurement.

MATERIALS:

Rulers, yardsticks, measuring tapes, paper, pencil, butcher paper and a large floor area, such as a hallway or gymnasium.

PROCEDURE:

1. Tell the class that they are going to draw a giant Gulliver figure on rolled butcher paper that is twelve times the average height of the student body. (The Lilliputians were one-twelfth the height of Gulliver.)

2. As a math experience ask the students to figure out the average height of their classmates.

3. Next, ask students to figure out how tall the Gulliver giant figure would have to be if it were twelve times as tall as their average height.

4. Ask for volunteers to measure and draw Gulliver on the basis of the above figures.

5. Cut out the giant figure.

6. Ask for more volunteers to act as tailors, and measure Gulliver for an entire suit of clothes using rulers, yardsticks and measuring tapes. Remind students to get a measurement for the sleeve, pant leg, neck and head.

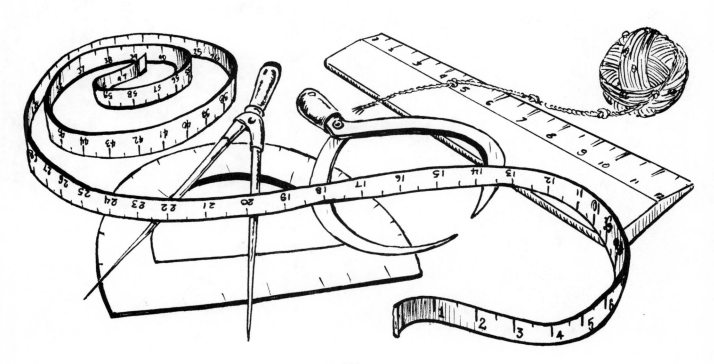

BACKWARDS ACADEMY OF LAPUTA

OBJECTIVES:

1. To help students relate to Swift's commentary on reason.

2. To help students understand the "folly" of the characters who inhabit Balnibarbi.

3. To introduce the scientific method, and to give students the opportunity to work with it.

4. To offer experiences in role playing.

MATERIALS: Paper, pencil, cucumber, ice, wafers, and classroom materials that could be used to construct a miniature house, like cardboard, toothpicks, etc.

PROCEDURE:

1. Review the five steps in the scientific method:
   a. Hypothesis: an educated "guess" stating what you hope to prove.
   b. Materials: all items required to perform your experiment.
   c. Procedures: all steps in the experiment in order, i.e., how do you conduct your experiment?
   d. Results: what happened when you did your experiment?
   e. Conclusions: discuss the success or failure of your experiment and why you felt it proved or disproved your hypothesis.

2. Tell students that they will now become Balnibarbians in the Grand Academy working to prove what Gulliver's hosts were working on in their laboratory.

3. Divide the class into four groups. Ask each group to select one experiment to do from the following:
   a. Removing sunshine from cucumbers.
   b. Making gunpowder from ice.
   c. Teaching mathematics by feeding wafers. (Teacher may wish to explain control and experimental groups to students.)
   d. Building a house from the roof down.

4. Each group must perform the experiment in a scientific fashion, write it up, and draw conclusions.

5. Each group of scientists could share their conclusions with the class.

THE LILLIPUTIANS TAKE A POCKET INVENTORY

OBJECTIVES:

1. To illustrate how one's tools, artifacts and possessions reveal information about one's life and times.

2. To give each student the opportunity to reflect how to represent his life via concrete objects.

MATERIALS: Collections of selected possessions brought from home by each student.

PROCEDURE:

1. Review the items that the Lilliputians found in Gulliver's pockets: scimitar, pocket pistols, pouch of powder and bullets, watch, silver and copper money, purse with nine large pieces of gold, knife, razor, comb, silver snuffbox, handkerchief and journal book.

2. Discuss what these items tell about Gulliver's mental and physical habits, personality, background and occupation.

3. Ask the students to bring in a collection of personal possessions which would represent their lives and times if they were to be placed in a time capsule.

4. Ask each student to bring the collection to class in a sack labelled with the owner's name. Reveal the contents of each sack one at a time without revealing its owner. Ask the class to guess the name of the owner of each sack via relating the collected items to the habits and interests of classmates.

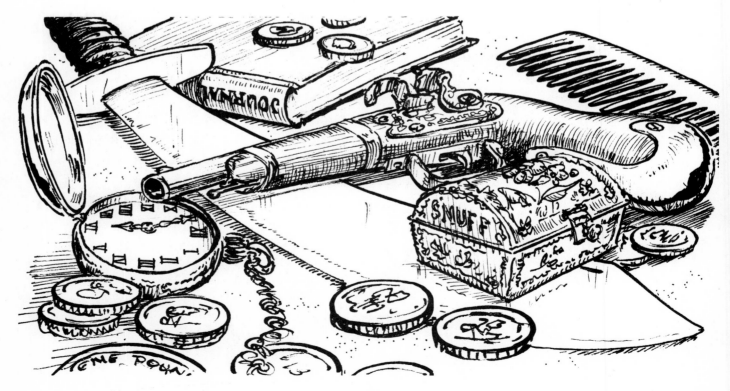

MIDGET LANDS IN BROBDINGNAG

OBJECTIVES:
1. To help students relate to the unique characteristics of the second island that Gulliver visits.
2. To help students understand the adventure inherent in Gulliver's travels, especially on Brobdingnag.
3. To help students explore a point of view through role playing.

MATERIALS: Paper, pencil, tape recorder, microphone, table and simulated TV cameras, and radio broadcasting microphones (optional).

PROCEDURE:
1. This activity could be used after Book III in *Gulliver's Travels*. Briefly review the "musts" in any type of news reporting including who, what, where, when, how, etc. The teacher should decide whether the news should take the form of a TV, radio, or newspaper account. If TV, remind students to film representative shots. If radio, remind students to verbalize in order to build interest.

2. As Gulliver lands on Brobdingnag, he arrives in a land of giants. Students in your classroom should be asked to imagine what the giants felt and thought when they saw this little man. Students should be asked to pretend that they are the giants and must report the "alien's arrival" and the circumstances surrounding his landing. The news report should be delivered from the point of view of the islanders (i.e., MIDGET LANDS). Students could then select one portion of Gulliver's experiences on the island and report it to all the home viewers and listeners.

3. Photos, maps, and graphs could accompany the report depending upon the vehicle the teacher chooses to use. The news report could be presented to the class.

118

AROUND THE WORLD WITH GULLIVER

OBJECTIVES:

1. To make the students aware of the various settings in *Gulliver's Travels*.
2. To help students understand the political, social, and physical aspects of the story.

MATERIALS:

Paper, pencil, poster board, colored construction paper, crayons, markers, art supplies.

PROCEDURE:

1. Gulliver, an apparently average 18th century man, visits four unique environments. Each of these settings includes unique social, physical and political atmospheres. Throughout the book, the characters he meets help him learn about human nature. Your students' ages and maturity levels will dictate the amount of satire and politics they can glean from the travels.

   Book I   Gulliver lands in Lilliput, a land of 6" tall humans. This down-scaled world is filled with adventure. Gulliver is honored with the title of " nardac," befriends the queen, fights a battle and "escapes" charges of treason. In this world, Swift comments upon politicians and politics.

   Book II   Gulliver visits Brobdingnag, a land of giants. Here Gulliver is treated as an "exhibit" piece, and is carried around in a cage-like structure. Swift uses this book to comment upon morality.

   Book III   Gulliver arrives on Balnibarbi, a floating cloud. He meets the Laputans who think very abstractly about scientific and mathematical principles. Most of the island has astrological orientations. Here Swift comments upon reason and intellect.

   Book IV   Gulliver's last stop is a visit with the Houyhnhnms and the Yahoos, horses and creatures (uncivilized). Here Gulliver must adjust his eating habits and life-style again. Swift comments upon man and sin.

2. Each island has a "lure" for Gulliver. Discuss this "lure" with your students. Then divide the class into four groups, assigning one island to each group.

3. Tell each group that they will be travel agents, and must "lure" their customers to their assigned island. Each group should be encouraged to make maps, brochures, posters, packing aids, etc., so that potential travellers can be prepared for each particular island.

4. These travel "agents" could then present their travel folders and recommendations to the class.

THE LAPUTAN FAST FOOD CHAIN

OBJECTIVES:

1. To experience the folly of the Laputan preoccupation with mathematical shapes and musical symbols.
2. To experience an opportunity to develop the imagination.
3. To review geometric forms and introduce others depending on the grade level.

MATERIALS: Drawing paper, pencils, rulers, markers, protractors and compasses.

PROCEDURE:

1. Discuss the Laputan preoccupation with mathematical and musical shapes and symbols. Bring out the fact that this preoccupation had no practical application. Consequently, it had no meaning and no use.
2. Review the dinner that the king had delivered to Gulliver:
   a. a shoulder of mutton cut into an equilateral triangle
   b. a piece of beef cut into a rhomboid
   c. a pudding in the shape of a cycloid
   d. two ducks trussed up into the shape of a fiddle
   e. sausages and puddings looking like flutes
   f. bread cut into cones, cylinders and parallelograms.
3. Divide the class into groups of three or four. Ask each group to design a menu for a Laputan fast food restaurant. This design must include a picture of each item drawn in either a mathematical shape or musical symbol. Encourage the group to use imagination in verbally describing each entry, also.
4. Share the menus with all the groups.

TRUE AND FALSE QUESTIONNAIRE
GULLIVER'S TRAVELS

1. Lilliputians were tiny humans no more than six inches high.

2. In Brobdingnag, Gulliver is a midget, and is treated as a museum piece on display.

3. The Houyhnhnms and the Yahoos were Lilliputians who helped Gulliver escape from Brobdingnag.

4. The Laputans are concerned with science and math.

5. Lemuel Gulliver is an English doctor who visits six islands and recounts his adventures in *Gulliver's Travels.*

6. Jonathan Swift was Gulliver's best friend.

7. All subjects were commanded to break eggs at the small end only in Lilliput.

8. In Lilliput, Gulliver marries the farmer's daughter and becomes king of the island.

9. People who inhabit the flying island are called Yahoos.

10. Laputans kept law and order on their island by dropping stones on citizens in rebellion.

11. All the people Gulliver met in his travels liked him instantly and made Gulliver feel at home on their island.

12. When Gulliver was captain of a ship, some seamen he recruited turned out to be buccaneers and chained Gulliver in his cabin.

13. In Houyhnhnm land, Gulliver learns to eat oat paste, milk, rabbits, birds and herbs.

14. In Laputa, Gulliver ate bread cut into cones and parallelograms.

15. Gulliver is charged with treason and sentenced to slow starvation in Lilliput.

16. In Brobdingnag, Gulliver falls in love with Glumdalclitch, the farmer's daughter, and is forbidden to marry her.

17. In Gulliver's pockets, the Lilliputians found things like cigars, money clips, photos of his family and a grocery list.

18. The Laputans were attempting to build a house from the roof down.

(1) T (2) T (3) F (4) T (5) F (6) F (7) T (8) F (9) F (10) T (11) F (12) T (13) T (14) T (15) T (16) F (17) F (18) T

JONATHAN SWIFT
1667-1745

BORN Jonathan Swift was born on November 30, 1667, in Dublin, Ireland.

FAMILY Swift's father, Jonathan Swift, Sr., was a lawyer. He died before Swift was born. His mother, Abigail Erick, was left with Jonathan and his older sister Jane. She was forced to return home and leave Swift to be raised by uncles.

CHILDHOOD Swift was well-educated for the times. His nurse had him reading by the age of three. He attended Kilhenny School and entered Trinity College at the age of fourteen. He was an avid reader. Swift worked on a Masters at Oxford University.

CONTRIBUTIONS Swift was a poet, a constant defender of Ireland, a member of the clergy and one of the most brilliant satirists the world has known.

INTERESTING FACT Swift was the cousin of John Dryden, English poet, dramatist and critic.

EPITAPH OR FINAL THOUGHT "Savage indignation no longer tears his heart." Swift died on October 19, 1745, in Dublin at the age of seventy-seven. At the end of his life, Swift concluded that he would have prospered socially and economically if he had not been so politically active with his satire.

JULIUS CAESAR

WILLIAM SHAKESPEARE

HOMECOMING

OBJECTIVES:

1. To help students understand the political theme which is evidenced throughout the play.

2. To make students aware of the characters, their alliances and their beliefs.

3. To help students understand why Caesar was assassinated.

4. To help students understand the fickle nature of the crowd in *Julius Caesar.*

MATERIALS:

White bed sheets to make banners, poles, crayons, markers, paints and poster board instead of sheets (optional).

PROCEDURE:

1. The play opens as Caesar returns with victory over Pompey's sons. Many of the "workmen" have gathered to honor him. Cassius and Brutus do not feel he should be honored, each for a different reason. On the other hand, Antony wishes to honor Caesar by offering him the crown.

2. Discuss this homecoming with the students, stressing not only the division between Antony-Caesar and Brutus-Cassius, but also Cassius' jealousy and Brutus' desire to "help" Rome. Also, point out Antony's friendship and respect for Caesar.

3. Then, ask the students to think about the Caesar-Antony philosophy. Students could simulate the homecoming celebration by making banners with slogans ("Yea Caesar," "Caesar the Victor," "Welcome Winner") writing songs and chanting welcome words. As Caesar arrives with Antony, students could form a procession to show their delight with their safe and victorious return.

4. This homecoming procession could be staged outdoors with all the appropriate cheers and chants. Some students may be cast as Caesar, Antony, Brutus, Calpurnia and Portia. Students should be reminded to stay in character.

5. Display banners in the room to remind students of the crowd's initial allegiance.

6. As an extension of this project, students may wish to construct banners and signs with slogans that depict allegiance to a modern day, political hero. Such parallels will require research.

FAMOUS LAST WORDS

OBJECTIVES:
1. To help students understand the sequence of events in *Julius Caesar.*

2. To remind students of the famous dialogue in *Julius Caesar.*

3. To give students an overview and review of the entire play.

MATERIALS: Paper, scissors, glue, poster board and crayons (optional).

PROCEDURE:
1. Once students have completed the play, list A through G (as shown in step 2) on the chalkboard. Have students copy each quotation on a separate sheet of paper.

2. Each statement represented could be discussed with students and verbally placed in context.

    a.   "Et tu, Brute!" - Caesar's dying words.

    b.   "Friends, Romans, countrymen" - Antony's speech at Caesar's funeral

    c.   "Cassius has a lean and hungry look" - Caesar states this prior to his assassination

    d.   "Beware the Ides of March" - the soothsayer's warning to Caesar as he goes to Senate

    e.   "For Brutus is an honourable man" - the theme of Antony's eulogy for Caesar

    f.   "This was the noblest Roman of them all" - Antony says this about Brutus after Brutus dies

    g.   "Thou shalt see me at Philippi" - the ghost of Caesar speaks to Brutus before the battle.

3. Ask students to place the quotes on poster board in sequence from the order of events in the play. Students might be encouraged to fill in other events either in words or pictures between the quotes. This will give students a pictorial overview of *Julius Caesar.*

TABLEAU OF CONSPIRACY

OBJECTIVES:

1. To visually understand the assassination scene.

2. To study the characterization of each of the participants in the conspiracy in order to link inner motives with physical features, i.e., posture and facial expression.

MATERIALS:

Five white sheets for togas, a laurel wreath for Caesar, camera and film and the accompanying illustration.

PROCEDURE:

1. Define the word *conspiracy* as being an agreement between people who ban together in order to cause an illegal or evil act.

2. Identify the major conspirators as follows:
   Brutus, a well-respected nobleman who murders Caesar for what he believes is the good of the state; *Cassius*, a practical man and schemer who murders Caesar out of personal envy and jealousy; *Casca*, an excitable, blunt and rude man who enters into the conspiracy out of admiration for Brutus; *Metellus Cimber*, a revengeful man who uses the question of his brother's banishment to get physically close to Caesar on the day of the assassination.

3. Using the accompanying illustration, stage a frozen picture of the conspirators at the Senate with Caesar.
   Metellus is on his knees asking for Caesar to repeal his brother's banishment. Remind the student portraying Metellus to use exaggerated humility as he makes this fake request in order to come physically close to Caesar. *Casca* is standing behind Caesar. He excitedly strikes the first blow aiming at the back of Caesar's neck. *Cassius* is crowded around Caesar. He instigated the plot and should be portrayed facially as cunning and envious. He is said to have "a lean and hungry look." *Brutus* is also crowded around Caesar. He is of noble birth and carries himself with style and dignity. His posture is erect and his head is held high. *Caesar* should be in the middle of the conspirators with his hand on Brutus' shoulder. His face should reveal his pain at being betrayed by his "angel" as he starts to collapse.

4. All participants should be dressed in togas. Take an instant developing picture of the frozen picture so that the students can see how close they came to duplicating the illustration.

5. Recast the tableau a number of times so that every student has the opportunity to participate.

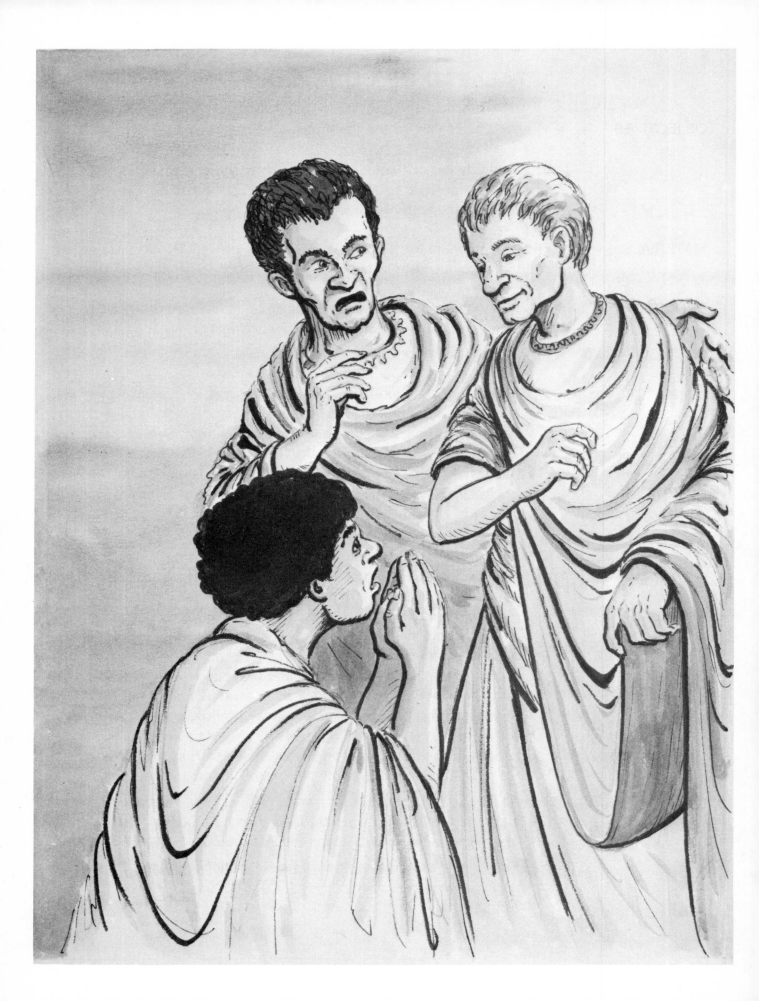

A GHOSTLY WALK THROUGH PHILIPPI

OBJECTIVES:

1. To become aware of the reaction of Brutus to a visit by Caesar's Ghost.

2. To become aware of Caesar's spirit and the effect it had on the battlefield.

3. To experience creative movement.

MATERIALS:

A large white sheet for the Ghost, a large empty room, cardboard pieces for the construction of shields, aluminum foil, markers, a drum, and the accompanying illustration.

PROCEDURE:

1. Discuss how Brutus felt after having been visited in his tent by Caesar's Ghost. Does Brutus not think this dream-visit to be a type of omen predicting the outcome of the battle?

2. After reviewing the Ghost's declaration that he will meet Brutus at Philippi, have the students construct battle shields. Brutus' soldiers should construct their shields out of cardboard and cover them with aluminum foil, whereas Antony's men should draw the seal of Caesar on theirs.

3. Stage a battle in slow motion to the beat of a drum. Soldiers of both armies should move offensively and defensively to the slow and steady beat.

4. Caesar's Ghost will also move across the battlefield in slow motion. As he moves, he should tap all of Brutus' soldiers on the shoulder one at a time. As each soldier is touched by Caesar's spirit, he should stop fighting and fall motionless to the floor. This should continue until Brutus' forces are all defeated.

5. Students should be reminded about their body movement: the Ghost could float in a light airy manner with the aid of a body extension such as a sheet; the soldiers could fall as if melting into the earth.

6. If equipment is available, the teacher may wish to tape the scene and play it back for the students. Some students may wish to create a sound track of battlefield noises by making their own sound effects. Allow each student wishing to portray Caesar's Ghost the opportunity to do so.

THE CRYSTAL BALL

OBJECTIVES:

1. To help students understand the significance of omens and the soothsayer in *Julius Caesar*.
2. To help students become aware of the use of "foreshadowing" in literary masterpieces.
3. To reinforce the basic plot of *Julius Caesar*.
4. To make students aware of vivid characterizations in the play.

MATERIALS:

Paper, pencil, crystal ball and tape recorder (optional).

PROCEDURE:

1. Throughout the play, characters are made aware of many omens, portents and predictions about the future. The teacher might point out some of these omens and the significance of the soothsayer who foretells the future by interpreting signs of nature. Examples include:
   - the soothsayer's warning "Beware the Ides of March"
   - Calpurnia's dream of Caesar's murder
   - turbulent weather prior to the "Ides"
   - "the lean and hungry look" of Cassius
   - Cassius believing that the battle on his birthday means his life has come full circle.

2. Point out to students that while we do not have soothsayers today, we do have fortune tellers, mystics, and people who predict the future based on planetary positions. Tell students that they will now tell the "future." Based upon their knowledge of the play, students will write horoscopes for various characters.

3. The teacher could select any act in the play. For example, write horoscopes for:
   - Caesar, Antony, Cassius and Brutus before the Ides of March
   - Cassius, Brutus, and Antony after the Ides
   - Portia, Cassius, Brutus and Antony just before the battle
   - the Ghost of Caesar before he visits Brutus in his tent

4. OPTIONAL: The teacher may wish to set up a fortune telling table and have various "characters" visit the teller.

MARK ANTONY'S INCREDIBLE IRONIC CHORUS

OBJECTIVES:

1. To establish a feel for what irony actually means.

2. To gain an understanding of how brilliant Mark Antony's speech was.

3. To study techniques of persuasive speaking.

4. To experience the auditory joy of participating in choral reading.

MATERIALS: Adaptation of Mark Antony's speech and a tape recorder.

PROCEDURE:

1. Discuss the scene as Mark Antony comes before the mob to speak. Highlight the fact that Antony is speaking in front of a totally hostile group; that he speaks with the consent of Brutus; and that Brutus has just spoken to the crowd and has left after having totally convinced them that Caesar's assassination was justified. Stress the point that Antony here puts his life in danger for his dead friend.

2. Read the adapted speech aloud to the students once to get their impressions.

3. Pass out copies of the adapted speech and ask the class to read aloud in unison with you. Point out the following techniques of persuasion:

   a. **appeal to patriotism**
   Antony constantly addresses the crowd as "countrymen." He reminds them, too, that Caesar filled the "general coffers."

   b. **appeal to emotions**
   Antony asks the crowd to bear with him because his heart is overcome with grief and he must pause a minute. He furthers the emotionality by using a most persuasive visual aid - Caesar's bloody body. And if that is not enough, he goes on to label the dagger wounds with conspirators' names.

   c. **appeal via the plain man technique**
   Antony establishes the feeling that he is an ordinary man just as they are with such lines as "I am no orator, as Brutus is; but, as you know me all, a plain blunt man."

   d. **appeal to greed**
   Antony cleverly lets it slip that Caesar has a will in which every citizen has been bequeathed something.

e. **appeal to the power of suggestion**

Throughout the speech Antony suggests the course of action to be taken without actually telling the crowd what to do. In this way the ideas are those of the crowd and not Antony's.

"If you have tears, prepare to shed them now."

"If the people were to hear this testament which, pardon me, I do not mean to read, they would go and kiss Caesar's wounds."

"But were I Brutus, and Brutus Antony, I would ruffle up your spirits and put a tongue in every wound of Caesar that would move the stones of Rome to rise and mutiny."

f. **appeal to the power of irony**

Antony's use of the word "honorable" as an adjective describing Brutus and the rest is most effective. It is repeated eight times in the adapted version of the speech. Eventually the word is so linked with dishonorable acts that it completely changes the meaning of the word to its opposite definition.

"I fear I wrong the honorable men whose daggars have stabbed Caesar."

4. Assign parts as prescribed by the adaptation. Rehearse individual parts before putting the entire adaptation together.

ANTONY #1:

Friends, Romans, countrymen, lend me your ears! I come to bury Caesar, not to praise him. The evil that men do lives after them, the good is often interred with their bones...so let it be with Caesar. The noble Brutus has told you Caesar was ambitious...If it were so, it was a grievous fault, and grievously has Caesar paid for it. Here, with permission of Brutus and the rest, **for Brutus is an honourable man, so are they all honourable men**...I come to speak at Caesar's funeral. He was my friend, faithful and just to me; but Brutus says he was ambitious, **and Brutus is an honourable man**. Caesar has brought many captives home to Rome, whose ransoms did the general coffers fill. Does this in Caesar seem ambitious?

ANTONY #2:

When the poor has cried, Caesar has wept! Ambition should be made of sterner stuff; yet Brutus says he was ambitious, and **Brutus is an honourable man**. You all do remember that I three times presented him with a kingly crown, which he did three times refuse! Was this ambition? Yet Brutus says he was ambitious, **and surely Brutus is an honourable man**! I speak not to disprove what Brutus spoke, but here I am to speak what I do know. You all did love him once, not without cause! What cause withholds you then to mourn for him? Bear with me, my heart is in the coffin there with Caesar, and I must pause till it comes back to me.

FIRST CITIZEN:

There is much reason in his sayings.

SECOND CITIZEN:

Caesar did not take the crown; therefore he was not ambitious!

THIRD CITIZEN:

There's not a nobler man in Rome than Antony!

FOURTH CITIZEN:

Listen! He begins to speak again!

ANTONY #3:

But yesterday, the word of Caesar might have stood against the world. Now he lies there, with no one to do him reverence. But here is a parchment with the seal of Caesar; I found it in his room. It is his will! If the people were to hear this testament which, pardon me, I do not mean to read, they would go and kiss Caesar's wounds, and dip their handkerchiefs in his sacred blood!

FIFTH CITIZEN:

The Will! The Will! We will hear Caesar's Will!

ANTONY #1:

Have patience, gentle friends, I must not read it. It is not proper that you should know how much Caesar loved you. You are not wood, you are not stones, but men! And being men, hearing the will of Caesar, it will inflame you, it will make you mad. It is good that you don't know that you are his heirs, for if you should, oh, what would come of it?

SIXTH CITIZEN:

We will hear the will, Antony! You shall read us the will!

ANTONY #1:

I shouldn't have told you about the will. **I fear I wrong the honourable men whose daggers have stabbed Caesar**; I do fear it!

SEVENTH CITIZEN:

Honourable men? They were traitors!

ALL CITIZENS:

The Will! The Testament!

EIGHTH CITIZEN:

They were villains…murderers! Read the Will!

ANTONY #1:

You will compel me then to read the Will?

ALL CITIZENS:
The Will! The Will! The Will! The Will!

ANTONY #2:
Then let me show you him that made the will. (Descends from pulpit and stands by Caesar's body.) If you have tears, prepare to shed them now. Look, in this place ran Cassius' dagger through. See what a rent the envious Casca made! Through this, the well-beloved Brutus STABBED. And as he plucked his cursed steel away, see how the blood of Caesar followed it, for Brutus, as you know, was Caesar's angel. This was the unkindest cut of all! For when the noble Caesar saw him stab, then burst his mighty heart.

NINTH CITIZEN:
O noble Caesar! Traitor's...Villains! We will be revenged!

ALL CITIZENS:
Revenge! Burn! Kill! Let Not a Traitor Live!

ANTONY #3:
Stay countrymen. Good friends, sweet friends, let me not stir you up to a sudden mutiny. **They that have done this deed are honourable.** Alas, I don't know what made them do it. **They are wise and honourable** and will no doubt tell you their reasons. I come not, friends, to steal away your hearts; I am no orator as Brutus is, but as you know me all, a plain, blunt man that loved my friend. For I have neither wit nor words, nor the power of speech, to stir men's blood. I only show you Caesar's wounds, poor, poor dumb mouths, and bid them speak for me. But were I Brutus, and Brutus Antony, I would ruffle your spirits and put a tongue in every wound of Caesar that would move the stones of Rome to rise and mutiny! (adapted by Henry K. Martin)

TRUE AND FALSE QUESTIONNAIRE
JULIUS CAESAR

1. Before Mark Antony spoke, Brutus had convinced the crowd that Caesar's assassination was justified.
2. Brutus reminds the crowd about Caesar's will.
3. Mark Antony's speech is very famous because of his clever use of the persuasion techniques.
4. Casca strikes the first blow at Caesar, aiming for the back of Caesar's neck.
5. When Caesar returns with a victory over Pompey's sons, Cassius wishes to honor Caesar with the crown.
6. The soothsayer foretells the future by interpreting signs of nature.
7. Julius Caesar did not heed the soothsayer's warning to "Beware the Ides of March."
8. Antony believed that Brutus was an honorable man.
9. Cassius, Brutus and Antony plotted to kill Caesar.
10. Portia was Caesar's wife.
11. Calpurnia warned Caesar not to leave the house on the day of the assassination.
12. The ghost of Shakespeare visits Brutus in his tent to warn Brutus of impending death.
13. Mark Antony convinced Caesar to go to the Senate on the day of his assassination.
14. Casca begged Caesar to repeal his brother's banishment.
15. Just before Caesar fell, he uttered the words, "Et tu, Brute?"
16. Cassius warned Brutus not to allow Antony to speak at the funeral.
17. Cassius had "a lean and hungry look."
18. The armies of Brutus-Cassius and Antony-Octavius met in Macedonia.
19. Brutus wanted to meet the enemy but Cassius wanted the enemy to seek them.

(1) T (2) F (3) T (4) T (5) F (6) T (7) T (8) F (9) F (10) F (11) T (12) F (13) F (14) F (15) T (16) T (17) T (18) F (19) T

WILLIAM SHAKESPEARE
1564 - 1616

BORN Shakespeare was born in April, 1564, in the medieval community of Stratford in Warwickshire, England.

FAMILY Shakespeare's father, John Shakespeare, was in the glove-making business. His mother was Mary Arden. Shakespeare had three brothers and two sisters.

CHILDHOOD At seven years of age, Shakespeare attended the Stratford Grammar School. Classes were in session from 7:00 a.m. to 5:00 p.m. The subjects taught were reading, writing and Latin. His free time was probably spent viewing the circus, travelling fairs and touring acting troupes. It is thought that he was writing poetry by the time he was sixteen.

CONTRIBUTIONS Shakespeare is considered the greatest playwright the world has ever produced. In total he wrote thirty-eight plays. These plays have been produced continually since they made their debut approximately four hundred years ago.

INTERESTING FACT Although Shakespeare had three children, they were not able to keep the bloodline from dying. His son Hamnet died. Hamnet's twin sister, Judith, did bear two sons of her own, but one died in infancy and the other died at the age of twenty-one, leaving no children. Shakespeare's eldest daughter, Susanna, did give birth to a daughter named Elizabeth. Elizabeth was the last of Shakespeare's bloodline to survive as she had no children.

EPITAPH OR FINAL THOUGHT
Good friend, for Jesus' sake forbear
To dig the dust enclosed here
Blest be the man who spares these stones,
And curst be he that moves my bones.